# DICK JONES
## Where the Action Was

### Ann Snuggs

*Ann Snuggs*

*June 2016*

Back cover photo: The author with Betty and Dick Jones at the 2010 Memphis Film Festival. (Photo by Frances Taylor)
Dick Jones: Where the Action Was
By Ann Snuggs

Published in the USA by:
BearManor Media

P O Box 71426
Albany, Georgia 31708
www.bearmanormedia.com

ISBN: 978-1-59393-891-8
Printed in the United States of America
Cover design by Ann Snuggs
Book design by Robbie Adkins, www.adkinsconsult.com

# Table of Contents

This book is dedicated to
Dick and Betty Jones.

# Acknowledgements

First of all, working on a book like this would never have occurred to me without Betty and Dick Jones. Betty suggested that Dick and I work to preserve his memories and pushed Dick for years to get him to talk. I am indebted to Dick for finally agreeing to share stories, giving me copies of his collection of stills and for just being Dick Jones, a good friend and special person.

Along the trail many others contributed in a variety of ways. I appreciate each and every one and could never manage to name them all.

A number of people helped me locate videos. Special thanks to Dwight Morrow, Mike Brady, Terry Swindol, Boyd Magers, Eddie Bishop and Gerard Noland.

Writers could never do their work without readers. Thanks to those who read the pieces as they were finished and made suggestions, Sue Winsor, Becky Taylor and, as always, Kristofer Todd Upjohn, who has been reading and editing my manuscripts from the first publication.

Thanks to my friend Frances Taylor, who took the special photograph of me with Dick and Betty Jones.

I owe deep appreciation to Mr. and Mrs. Elvin Sweeten of the Gene Autry Oklahoma Museum, who allowed me to take pictures of the Dick Jones exhibit, and Johnny Western, Dick's good friend, who wrote the forward.

Very special thanks to Boyd and Donna Magers, who have supported this project from the first discussions of its possibility.

# Forward: "Dick Jones Changed My Life" by Johnny Western

Dick Jones changed my life!

To understand how, we have to go back to my fifth birthday, October 28, 1939. I saw my first Gene Autry movie, *Guns and Guitars*, and decided that day I wanted to be just like him, never dreaming, as that young boy, that in 1956, he would put me under contract and take me on tour with him for the next two years.

To get to that point, I sang on the radio when I was thirteen and had my own radio show on KDHL in my hometown of Northfield, Minnesota, when I was fourteen. When I was sixteen, I had Gene Autry on my show as a guest. He said if I ever came to Hollywood to look him up.

When I was nineteen, I moved to North Hollywood and tried to get started in show biz out there. After living in the Valley for a few months, I heard Gene was filming at his Melody Ranch Studio and decided to drive out to see him. When I got there, I found out he had finished filming for the day but Dick Jones was filming *Buffalo Bill, Jr.* I had loved Dick in *The Range Rider* TV series, which I had seen in Minnesota.

Dick was not needed for a while on set. I introduced myself and told him about the invitation from Gene. We got to visit for about an hour before he had to go back to work. I gave him two of my records that I had intended to give to Gene and I gave him my phone number.

A few days later, he called me and said he really liked my voice and the records and to come out again and watch him film. I was working a day job to support my wife and six-month-old daughter but I got some time off and went back. We had another great visit and he asked me to go with him and Jock Mahoney to Sacramento, where they were doing a *Range Rider* personal appearance. They needed someone to handle and set up in the rodeo arena for the stunts they would be doing. It paid $50 a day and expenses. My first paid show biz job in California!

I was making $89.50 a week, take home, in my day job and they paid me $150 for that weekend.

From then on I visited with Dick and his wife Betty on a regular basis. Also with Jock Mahoney and his wife, actress Maggie Field, whose young daughter turned out to be movie star, Sally Field.

I kept my day job. The spring of 1956 rolled around and I got a call from Dick. He said he and Betty would be celebrating their eighth wedding anniversary in a few days and wanted me to sing at their party. So I did.

The party was at the Leonard Eilers Ranch in the San Fernando Valley and I would be singing for "a few friends." Dick did not tell me "friends" were Roy Rogers and Dale Evans, the Sons of the Pioneers and their family of folks. Also movie star Susan Hayward was there. So was Gene Autry with his wife Ina.

So I got my guitar and sang for about twenty minutes or so. Then Roy Rogers borrowed my guitar and had me stay on stage with them and sing some songs like "Cool Water" and "Tumbling Tumbleweeds." It went over really well and we all had a great time.

Two weeks later, Dick called me and said that Gene Autry wanted to see me at his office the next day. I called in sick and went to see Gene in Hollywood. He told me that my guitar hero, Johnny Bond, was retiring from his show after thirty years and he remembered what I had done at Dick and Betty's party. He offered me

*A young Johnny Western signed this still for Dick many years ago.*

$350 a week and all my expenses! Wow! The money and the job were unreal, plus getting to work with and for my hero!

When Gene semi-retired in 1957, he put me over with his agent, Mitch Hamilburg, who was also Dick's and Jocko's agent, as well as agent for Gail (*Annie Oakley*) Davis. Mitch got me my first movie role and my career took off from there. All because Dick Jones called me to sing at his party!

In 1960-'61, Dick was doing well in the real estate business, as well, and found us a house in Canoga Park, California. During the time we lived there, I did my last film called, *The Night Rider*.

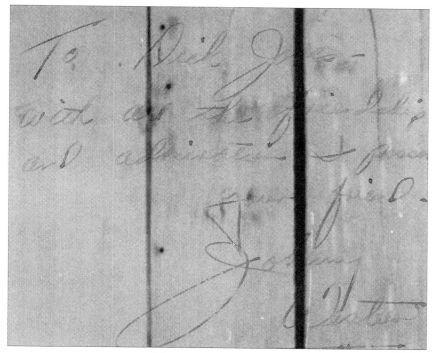

*Close-up of the inscription.*

The film starred Johnny Cash, with whom I had been touring and recording since 1958, after Gene retired. The theme song of the movie was Cash's big hit, "Don't Take Your Guns to Town." Dick Jones played the role of Billy Joe, on which the song was based.

I would continue to work with Johnny Cash for the next three and one half decades, for a total of forty years.

Dick went into real estate full time and we didn't see each other for many years. I had been singing at my favorite film festivals across the country and was booked in the town of Gene Autry, Oklahoma, for their annual festival. And, lo and behold, when I got there, the first person I saw was Dick Jones! So many years since we had seen each other!

Then, as luck would have it, Dick and I worked many film festivals across America for many more years. He, my wife Jo, and his wife Betty had so much fun and did so many things together right up until the time we lost him.

So, you seem Dick Jones changed my life. Had he not invited me to sing at that party, my life with Gene Autry would have never happened. And my life with Gene and Dick led to my TV and movie career and led to my writing and singing the theme song to one of the biggest television series of all time, *Have Gun Will Travel* on CBS. This led to my second contract with Columbia Records.

Dick Jones and I have our tiles in the Walkway of the Stars in the courtyard of the Autry Museum in Hollywood. Dick's says, "He rode the silver screen with Gene Autry." Mine says, "He owes it all to Gene Autry."

In my mind, I owe it all to Gene AND Dick Jones.

# Introduction

Many a good story begins with, "once upon a time."

Once upon a time, make that February 25, 1927, in Snyder, Texas, a baby boy was born, Richard Percy Jones. Young Dickie learned to ride about the same time he learned to walk and by the time he was four years old, the family had moved to McKinney and he was performing a specialty act at rodeos. Billed as "The World's Youngest Trick Rider and Trick Roper," Dickie's horsemanship caught the eye of cowboy film star, Hoot Gibson, who said he should be in pictures.

Before he could blink, Dickie was on his way to Tinseltown and staying at Hoot's ranch while he trained for a film career. The versatile young actor played many major stars "as a boy" or often essayed the role of the brother of the hero's sweetheart. He was in great demand for Westerns because he could do his own riding.

Fast forward almost twenty years.

After serving in World War II, Dickie returned to Hollywood. Gene Autry noted his talent, especially for action roles, and hired him to be in several pictures.

Action! That was the key to attracting the juvenile audience. Now using the more grown-up name, "Dick," Jones was just the man to deliver it.

Western movies and television shows have always been action-packed. It's the nature of the beast. So when Autry organized Flying A Productions and began producing television shows about the West, Dick was a natural to be hired. The shows would focus on action. His first regular role for Flying A was on *The Range Rider*.

Nowadays filmed entertainment is filled with CGI (computer-generated image) special effects. Stunt work is enhanced by technology.

In the early days of television, that action was totally dependent upon the skill and athleticism of the performers. The talents of Dick Jones and Jock Mahoney, Dick's partner on *The Range Rider*, were some of the finest to ever grace the industry.

As a result, the two series of the 1950s in which Dick had a starring role contained the most footage of action sequences of the era. *Buffalo Bill, Jr.* as well as *The Range Rider* was made by Gene Autry's Flying A Productions, which also produced the juvenile-audience aimed *The Gene Autry Show*, *The Adventures of Champion* and *Annie Oakley*. Autry understood the value of action.

*The Range Rider* ran from 1951 to 1953, seventy-eight episodes. Jock played the Range Rider and Dick portrayed his teenage sidekick and saddle partner, Dick West.

Some fine stuntmen shared the set with Jones and Mahoney, as well as a group of actors who were capable of doing their own fight work and minor action. Many of the personnel have said time and again in interviews that working on those shows was a favorite memory in the course of their careers.

The episodes were shot at Pioneertown, two per week. It was almost like going to an intensive activity camp. The atmosphere was congenial overall and the product of that activity was outstanding.

*Buffalo Bill, Jr.* ran a season and a half, forty-two episodes, in 1955-1956. In that series, Dick had no skilled partner as a regular. The action depended upon him working with the fine group of stuntmen and action actors who worked for the Flying A. It did not slow him down.

This story of the television segment of the career of Dick Jones begins with a look at the supporting players of these two shows, here nicknamed the Flying A Stock Company.

# Flying A Stock Company

Like any number of directors and/or producers, Gene Autry preferred working with those he knew and in whose abilities he had confidence.

When Flying A shows were being staffed, whether in front of or behind the cameras, people with a proven track record were hired again and again. They became, in effect, a stock company. Just as noted director John Ford had his famous crew, so did Gene Autry.

For the two-a-week filmed television shows this was extremely convenient.

As Dick said:

*Range Riders were often made with the same group of actors. We'd go up to Pioneertown and every week they'd bring us a new batch of actors. The actors they'd bring up were cast in two parts. They'd be doing one part in one episode and another in another episode and we'd make two in a week. Not simultaneously but the fewer camera angles they made, the cheaper it was to do, so they might just turn the camera angle ten degrees and you got a new set, and they'd bring in a couple of actors that had changed their clothes.*

He compared it to the early B-Westerns.

*Like in the early days of Westerns they'd have a posse chasing the outlaws, right to left. Then they'd get to the end and turn around, change their hats and paint some spots on the horses and go back the other direction, left to right, and you've got the posse chasing itself. You use the same actors with different hats and, to the eye, different horses. Use a bay horse going right to left and a spotted horse going the other way after you paint some spots on him.*

Probably the first to become part of the unofficial stock company were the behind-the-scenes group, directors and crew.

A name that goes back to some of Dick's first lines on screen was part of Flying A from its origin, Armand "Mandy" Schaefer. Schaefer both directed and contributed to the screenplay for *Burn 'Em Up Barnes*, the first serial in which Dick spoke lines. Dick had also worked with Schaefer on Gene Autry films and television shows.

Dick admired him and respected his abilities.

*Mandy Schaefer was about the best at putting low-budget pictures together. He made his name famous at Republic with all the serials and Westerns they were shooting. He did about ninety percent of Gene Autry's films so when Gene formed Flying A, Mandy Schaefer was one of the partners.*

*He was one of the best.*

Another name from the past who was a staple at Flying A was director George Archainbaud. French-born Archainbaud had worked in film since the days of silents and was also a veteran of Gene Autry films.

Dick had compliments for him, too.

*He was good. He was the best director that Autry had because he would edit it in the camera. That would save an awful lot of film getting thrown on the floor. He wouldn't waste it. He had all the camera angles, cuts and the stuff done in his book – in his head. He'd put it into the camera magazine and then the editors hardly had a job to do to put it together. They really liked him.*

An added note Dick remembered about Archainbaud was his name.

*George Archainbaud said the "d" in his name was silent like in "fish."*

*I said, "What!?"*

*He said, "How do you pronounce "d" in fish?"*

*I said, "You don't."*

*He said, "That's George Arch-in-baw."*

Another time Dick set Archainbaud straight.

*I used to upset George Archainbaud, the director, something ter-rible till he got to know me better. The first time I think I stepped off the right-hand side [of the horse] he said, "Cut! Cut!"*

*I said, "What's the matter?"*

*He said, "You got off on the wrong side."*

*I said, "There is no right or wrong side. I get off on the side where the camera is."*

*And he said, "Oh. Okay."*

*So from then on, whenever I got off or on, it was on the side close to the camera because I didn't want the horse hiding me. He never said anything after that.*

Two other directors stood out in Dick's mind, Ross Lederman and Frank McDonald.

*They [those three] were the best. They knew what they were do-ing and they were real good at action and real good at working on the set and good at handling the leading ladies, at getting them to do their job.*

Billed throughout his long career as David Lederman, D. Ross Lederman and Ross Lederman, the director had also helmed a film early in Dick's career, *Moonlight on the Prairie* with Dick Fo-ran. Dick was seven and a half years old when that shoot-'em-up was filmed. Lederman was an old pro with a reputation for turning out productions on time and under budget by the time he hooked up with Autry. He shot a number of Flying A episodes.

Frank McDonald came to film later than Archainbaud or Leder-man but also managed to direct Dick in an earlier film, *Mountain Rhythm* (1943).

Ray Nazarro, Wallace Fox and William Berke also directed regularly for Flying A. All three had long film careers, Berke having started as an actor in silents. These men also were excellent at turning out productions efficiently.

Writers were less steadily employed, though veteran Western writer Oliver Drake received noticeable credit as did Dwight Cummins, Eric Freiwald and Robert Schaefer.

Probably the first regular on-camera personnel to be hired after the stars, Dick and Jocko, were the stunt players. With the focus on action in *The Range Rider* and *Buffalo Bill, Jr.,* and *The Range*

*Bob Woodward (left) with Dick on the set of* Buffalo Bill, Jr. *From the costumes, Woodward is probably getting ready to drive for Dick in a chase scene. Dick said of him, "Bob Woodard was a real longtime stuntman. He did several Buck Jones [films]. He was around all the time. He could drive a six-up. Blind drive. He could do anything where a horse was concerned."*

*Rider* packed with the most action footage of any television show of the time, stuntmen were essential.

Long-time stuntman Bob Woodward has the most credits for the Flying A, but he was also uncredited in some episodes. He was another old-timer who had worked with Dick before, back in the days when Dick was playing the kid brother and Woodward was doubling Buck Jones in *Hollywood Round-Up* (1937).

Woodward was born in Oklahoma in 1909. His first film appearance was in a 1931 Tom Tyler film, *Rider of the Plains*. He doubled many top names and in the 1940s became a regular double for Gene Autry, along with Sandy Sanders.

Sanders was another Flying A regular. Dick called him, ". . . a photogenic double for Gene Autry, so Gene liked him."

Texan Sanders was performing a horse act in Kansas when a traveling film crew suggested his talents might be useful in Hollywood. Sanders soon became one of Gene Autry's doubles and worked in many films as both an actor and a stuntman.

Cowboy Boyd Stockman was also spotted by film people and encouraged to take his considerable skills in front of the camera. His familiar face is often seen at the reins of a stagecoach, as driving was one of his specialties.

He, too, doubled Autry and was a regular in Autry films and also for the Flying A. Dick said, "Boyd Stockman was the same [as Bob Woodward], but wasn't around the business as long as Bob was."

Woodward and Stockman were the regular blind drivers, a critical role in many of the action sequences in *The Range Rider* and *Buffalo Bill, Jr.* A blind driver is hidden in the wagon bed and has the actual control of the team. The actor on the wagon seat holds the reins but the blind driver holds the small, almost invisible reins that provide the real guidance for the horses.

Even though Donna Hall was considered a free-lancer, she worked a lot of action for Flying A. Dick phrased it this way:

> *We had a couple of real good stuntwomen because most of the women weren't riders. You could tell right off the bat if they were half-way handy on a horse because of the way they'd get on one. If they couldn't get on we knew we had to double.*

*This four picture sequence shows Dick bulldogging Al Wyatt from a horse and continuing the fall down a hill and likely into a fight.*

*The stuntwoman we used most was Donna Hall. And you see her on every one of the Annie Oakleys because she did the hippodrome coming through and shooting the target in the opening of the Annie Oakley shows. She did that in Madison Square Garden and Gene saw it and said come on out to Hollywood.*

With so many of the women having only a nodding acquaintance with horses, Donna was often on the set, dependable and capable of all that the men could do.

Expert horseman Al Wyatt played villains as well as did stunt work on *The Range Rider*. He was a highly respected stuntman in the business who moved up to stunt coordinator during his long career.

Dick and Jocko did their own stunts with a few exceptions that were brought about by unforeseen problems – and sometimes doubled other actors – but stunt players were essential to keep the action going. Dick held the stuntmen and -women in high esteem and counted a number of them as friends. He spoke of the company stunt players respectfully.

*Stuntmen that Gene had were like on contract. There were two or three, sometimes four, that were utilized for anything and everything. They always did it the easy way. Every now and then we'd get an actor that was hired because of his ability and he would turn in a good stunt. He was good at gags. There were three or four of those. We used those guys all the time. They were like a stock company.*

*Bob Woodward, Boyd Stockman. They were with Gene from the Republic days. He used them all the time and those guys could do anything. Either one of them could drive a six-up. They were good at wrecking wagons. They didn't do any wild saddle falls because they were protecting themselves but they had a plausible shot-out-of-saddle saddlefall. They were very handy at the fight scenes and knew camera angles.*

*Gene had his own stock company and we worked with them diligently and then Jocko brought in Fred Krone because he was a kid that wanted to learn the stunt business and he was very into it and very handy. He became one of the best stunt guys in the business.*

Fred Krone and Dick were close friends until Krone's death in 2010. Early in his career, Krone earned the nickname "Krunch" because he hit the ground so hard. He was well-liked and highly respected by his co-workers. He did a lot of credited and uncredited work for Flying A and worked with Jock Mahoney again on *Yancy Derringer.*

Just as the technical crew boasted years of experience, so did many of the actors. Many started in silents and made their last stands in the early years of episodic television, including Kermit Maynard, Bud Osborne, George J. Lewis, Tom London, Francis McDonald, Raymond Hatton, Lane Chandler, Edgar Dearing, Richard "Dick" Alexander and others.

Some skipped the silent era, performing on stage, in vaudeville and/or musical theater. Kenneth MacDonald, Lyle Talbot, Al Bridge, Dick Curtis, Terry Frost and more were among these.

Still others came from rodeo or had grown up around horses. Boyd "Red" Morgan, who had a good career as a stuntman, didn't remember not knowing how to ride [like Dick]. Bud Osborne, also experienced in stunts and teamster *par excellence*, was the same. Glenn Strange and Harry Lauter were among the rodeoers. George J. Lewis, Don C. Harvey, Kermit Maynard, Lane Chandler, Terry Frost, Ewing Mitchell and Myron Healey were early riders or simply good with horses. And Kenne Duncan was once a gentleman jockey in Canada.

One of the favorite familiar faces on Flying A shows was Stanley Andrews, who appeared in many episodes. Perhaps his face was so familiar because he played the Old Ranger who narrated *Death Valley Days*. He started in film in the early years of sound and was most often a benevolent character, though he made a terrific villain in *The Lone Ranger* (1938) serial.

More than once he and Dick shared screen credits, if not scenes, in films before *The Range Rider*. He worked for Flying A steadily, appearing in many episodes of both *The Range Rider* and *Buffalo Bill, Jr.*

Dick remembered him with warmth saying, "We protected him very well. He was an elderly man, an elderly gentleman. You could visualized him as the old prospector because when he played an old man he just acted himself. He was a good actor."

Gregg Barton was a comparative newcomer next to Andrews but he was a presence in the Flying A shows. He got his start by meeting an MGM casting director at a party and learned to ride horses to get the roles he wanted. In an interview with Tom and Jim Goldrup for *Feature Players, Volume 1*, he said he enjoyed working with the people in the Flying A stock company and also that he preferred the role of a baddie. He made a good one. Like other professional villains, he recognized that there are more roles for villains than for heroes.

Dick liked working with him and appreciated that, "Gregg Barton was a good fight guy. He didn't like to fight with me because he'd say every time he'd grab me by my shirt he'd get a handful of hair and rip the hairs out of my chest. Or maybe it was the other way around."

One of the popular stock company players was Harry Lauter. He came from a show business family. His grandparents were trapeze artists, the Flying Lauters. As a young man he both worked stock theater and rodeoed, giving himself a good background for work at the Flying A. He appreciated the quality of the stuntmen and became a good hand at handling action. When he spoke of those years he used the word, "fun."

Others thought him a bringer of that. In *Feature Players, Volume 4*, page 151, (2006) Alan Hale, Jr., another regular on the shows, mentioned Lauter in commenting on camaraderie on the set: "It was a delight to see people like Harry Lauter because you knew you were going to have a lot of fun."

Dick also remembered Harry as a good entertainer:

*He was all-around. Harry Lauter was one of the best. He was a fun guy. He had a sense of humor that just wouldn't quit. If we had any spare time – like we're on location sitting around after dinner – he'd start spinning yarns, telling stories and the next thing you know he's up acting them out. He was a hoot. He was a nice guy – a lot of fun to work with and very handy in fight scenes.*

*Oh, yeah, he was real good and a better rider than some.*

Lauter was another who preferred a role as a heavy.

One of the old-timers who frequented the Flying A shows was Tom London. He started in Chicago with Selig and moved to California with that company. In the silent era he was almost always a villain but made an easy transition to talkies where he played a variety of roles. He was credited in hundreds of parts during his long career.

Comfortable on a horse, he was handy in a crunch. Jennifer Holt said he once saved her life on a set by snatching her from the saddle as the horse she was riding went down.

By the time of *The Range Rider*, he was playing old codgers, prospectors, sheriffs and similar characters. Dick remembered him as "a good character actor." Regular watchers of Westerns will recognize his voice as quickly as his face.

George J. Lewis was another actor whose first appearances were in silents. He started as an extra, shifted to the New York stage when talkies came in, then went back to film in 1939.

One of his first films back in California was *Beware Spooks!* with Joe E. Brown. Interestingly, though they had no scenes together, Dick also had a small role in that film.

Lewis started in Westerns in the early 1940s and is best known for that genre. He had learned to ride as a young man and was comfortable on a horse.

Dick commented, when asked about a duel between the Range Rider and Lewis' character, "George was getting too old for that stuff [fencing]. He was in a lot of *The Range Riders*. Nice guy, too. He was very competent. Never had to retake because he flubbed his lines. He was a good mechanic."

Two other seasoned performers from the days of silent films who were seen in both *The Range Rider* and *Buffalo Bill, Jr.* were Edgar Dearing and Richard "Dick" Alexander. Dearing was nearly always cast as a sheriff at Flying A – often played for humor – while Alexander was a *mean* baddie. In the episode, "Hidden Gold," his character has a deliciously well-choreographed fight with the Range Rider.

One of the older players, who had actually not been working in film that long at the time of the Flying A shows, was William Fawcett. He had performed in stock companies after World War I, but became a teacher and held a PhD. During World War II, he went to California to work in the shipyards and stayed to try his hand at film acting at fifty-two years old. It was a good fit and he never looked back.

At the Flying A, he was usually cast as a crotchety character, one who added humor to the show. From the scaredy-cat cook running from the Range Rider and Dick's fake haunt to a neighboring store-owner sparring with Judge Ben "Fair and Square" Wiley, he played his characters to the hilt and entertained highly.

Old pro and versatile performer Glenn Strange was typecast at the Flying A. He played Indian chiefs in four different episodes. In his career, he was often a villain but could handle a wide array of roles – from musician to monster. His last, and most well-remembered, role for much of today's society was Sam, the bartender in *Gunsmoke*.

Don C. Harvey had not been in film many years before working for Flying A but had years of showbiz experience. As a young man he performed in traveling stock companies and on radio before moving to film.

Seems like almost every other episode, especially in the *Buffalo Bill, Jrs.*, there is James Griffith. With a face sure to gain plenty of work as the heavy, Griffith played Doc Holliday in a *Buffalo Bill, Jr.*, but his *Range Rider* appearances were usually on the wrong side of the law. A performer from kindergarten on, he was also a musician and screenwriter.

Music was part of the background for a number of the Flying

A stock company members. Myron Healey was a child singer on radio. He also played the violin and piano, and danced to boot. [He and Dick should have worked up a tap routine to entertain the crew.] He was good with horses and, like Harry Lauter and Alan Hale, Jr., enjoyed working with a familiar group of players.

John Doucette studied at Pasadena Playhouse and performed light opera. He also was a familiar figure in many television Westerns.

Henry Rowland started out in musical comedy and light opera. Light hardly describes his characters on *The Range Rider* and *Buffalo Bill, Jr.* An interesting note is that he played the German who led the German soldiers' singing in Rick's in *Casablanca* (1942).

Tom Monroe sang and was part of a dance band. In an interview in *Feature Players, Volume 1*, he talked about the good times at Pioneertown working on Flying A shows.

One of Denver Pyle's many jobs before he settled into acting was a drummer in a dance band. He was a fixture at Flying A, appearing in a large number of the episodes.

Ewing Mitchell was like the little girl with the curl, playing characters either very good or very bad. Most often he was a sheriff or marshal for the Flying A, albeit not the brightest one, but when he was bad he was truly horrid. He is best known as a lawman, Mitch, the sheriff on the television series, *Sky King*.

Mitchell came to film in the late forties from a stage career, but Westerns suited him well. He had a ranch and worked his own cattle.

Other good riders with B-Western experience included Kenne Duncan, Terry Frost and Dennis Moore. All were competent performers who could ride. Duncan traveled with a shooting exhibition; Frost started in vaudeville and worked in burlesque, as well as having riding ability and doing some fight work. Dennis Moore had performed on stage before becoming a familiar face in Western movies. Never let it be said that the performers in these shows were not versatile.

One who definitely did *not* get along with horses was Lyle Talbot, who made no bones about it. He did his best to avoid getting on a horse, though he played in plenty of Westerns. He had a stock company of his own in Memphis before going to California to perform in films.

House Peters, Jr. was a second generation film actor. He appeared in some Gene Autry films as well as being a regular on Flying A shows. In 1936, he played Frank Merriwell's chief adversary in the serial, *The Adventures of Frank Merriwell*. Young Dickie Jones also had a role in that cliffhanger.

Dick remembered him well:

*House Peters, Jr. was either a heavy or a townsman. I worked with him when he was even the juvenile love interest. He was versatile all right.*

*Did you know he used to be Mr. Clean? Every time I see that commercial, I just can't picture him. His voice is recognizable but I just can't visualize him bald-headed and all muscle-bound.*

Peters had a long career but Leonard Penn only worked in Westerns for ten years. During those he appeared in episodes of both *The Range Rider* and *Buffalo Bill, Jr.*, notably playing the father of Dick West in a couple of *Range Rider* shows.

Rodd Redwing was a full-blooded Chickasaw who taught shooting and knife-throwing to actors. His specialty show-off stunt was throwing a knife, then quickly shooting a hole in the wood for the knife to hit.

Redwing played Chief Young Eagle in *The Range Rider* episode, "Indian War Party." The script called for the chief and the Range Rider to fight. In the finished show, it's Dick, not Redwing doing the fighting.

Dick said:

*I doubled Rodd Redwing once when he was supposed to do a fight with Jocko. It was a* Range *Rider.*

*Jocko said, "We're gonna do this and we're gonna do that and we'll get up on this log and fall off the log and so on."*

*And Rodd said, "I didn't hire on to do that. I don't do stuff like that."*

*And Jocko said, "Well, you got to."*

*And I said, "Here, give me his costume and I'll double him. So we did a fight that scared everybody half to death. Under the horse, over the horse, over the log. The log was eight-foot high lying on the ground. Up on it and down it and around it. Had a lot of fun.*

*They almost sent Rodd Redwing home because he wasn't going to do that scene but I stepped in and said, "I'll do it for him."*

*We* [Dick and Jocko] *just changed the routine and did it real wild.*

Lee Van Cleef had been hired for *High Noon* (1952) and was taking jobs in the interim when he came to Flying A. Dick didn't

*At the end of the destructive fight in "Boomer's Blunder" Dick (center) has just returned Lee Van Cleef's gun. Nancy Gilbert (left) looks on.*

realize he was that new to the business and considered him professional and skilled.

*I liked working with Lee Van Cleef. He was a good fight man. He was fun to work with. He was a good actor.*

*I had a fight in the store in Wileyville with him. We tore that store up. Every shelf came down. Every table got turned upside down. We rode the barber chair around a couple of times. We demolished the store and at the very end I* [actually, it's Calamity] *hit him with a sack of flour and he ends up looking like Frosty, the Snowman.*

*Boyd Magers said, "That's the longest fight. Did you just do it as you went along?"*

*I said, "No. It took us almost all day long to choreograph that thing. We had so much to do. We had so many things to take care of. It was entirely choreographed. And Lee Van Cleef did his own stunts. He was very handy and I enjoyed working with him.*

*You can't risk not choreographing the fights. Someone might get hurt."*

Of all the women who worked for Flying A, only one made repeat appearances on both *The Range Rider* and *Buffalo Bill, Jr.*, Louise Lorimer.

Her role was usually a motherly type who turned out to be in league with the villains or the leader of the villains. She had a long career in a variety of roles, although she retired from film well before her death at age 97.

Quite a few of the Flying A regulars made multiple appearances in *The Range Rider* but were not in any episodes of *Buffalo Bill, Jr.*

One of the real cowboy old-timers was Bud Osborne. Born in Indian Territory in 1884, he was a rancher and Wild West Show performer who went to Hollywood with a stock consignment for silent director/producer Thomas Ince. His action skills and horsemanship helped him easily find work in talkies.

In his 50-year career he played villains, sheriffs, *segundos*, such as his role in *Blood on the Moon*, but is best known as a master teamster. He drove anything and everything. Wagons, buckboards, four-ups, six-ups. Look for him as the stagecoach driver in Flying

A shows. He was almost 70 at the time of *The Range Rider*.

Dick respected him saying, "Bud Osborne always made a good sheriff or stagecoach driver. He was a good character actor, good cowboy and good stage driver, too."

Another familiar face and voice was Kenneth MacDonald. He performed at eight years old. He sang tenor, was a noted high school athlete, did stage work in the 1920s and moved to film in the '30s. He specialized in slick villains. That dapper suit and tie amongst the boots and Western hats helped matinee audiences peg him immediately as the bad guy.

Though he appeared in many serials, he did not do action. He was an actor only, more than willing to keep the stuntman employed.

After all the years of villainy, in his later years he played a judge in thirty-two episodes of the *Perry Mason* television show. For Flying A, he became a good guy, too, playing a sheriff or marshal several times.

Al Bridge spent many an onscreen hour plotting the downfall of the man in the white hat and all the innocent townsfolk and ranchers struggling to build the Old West. His persona could move from slick to rough in order to achieve his evil goals.

By the time he got to *The Range Rider* he had mellowed into a sheriff, an old codger, comic relief. He came to film from a stock company where he managed and starred in musical comedies.

In *The Range Rider* episode, "Ten Thousand Reward," his hands noticeably reveal his age when they are shown counting the money.

Though he did not appear in any *Buffalo Bill, Jr.* episodes, his sister, Loie Bridge, played Mrs. Henley in the *Buffalo Bill, Jr.* episode, "Six-Gun Symphony."

Kermit Maynard was known as an all-round good guy in the business. Starting in silents, he doubled his brother Ken. He lettered in college sports, worked hard at becoming an expert on horseback and bought a dappled grey horse he named Rocky, whom he trained and used in winning trick and fancy roping at a National Competition Rodeo at Salinas.

In the mid-1930s, he starred in a series of B-Westerns. Dick played the little brother of the heroine in one of those, *Wild Horse Round-Up*.

Dick had the greatest respect for Maynard. He said that although Maynard is credited in no *Buffalo Bill, Jr.* episode, he was there.

> *Kermit Maynard was in about thirty percent of The* Range Riders *and at least twenty-five percent of the* Buffalo Bill, Jrs. *as a riding extra. Always in the background and very, very quiet. You wouldn't even know he was around. He was another nice guy. One of the good guys.*

Another seasoned old-timer who started in silents and appeared in many films and on television until his death was Raymond Hatton. He only made a few Flying A shows but did also work with Dick when he was a child.

Dick reminisced:

> *Raymond Hatton was one of the Rough Riders and was in some of the Three Mesquiteers pictures.*

> *I did the re-make* [feature film version] *of* Hi-Yo, Silver *[The Lone Ranger serial] – fifteen chapters. We did the segue between chapters and did it all in one day up at Lone Pine. Like the "tune in next week and see if the Lone Ranger can save Buddy from going over the cliff," or something like that.*

> *Instead of having a re-run of the last chapter, we would do that on the set. He would say, "Do you remember so-and-so and tell him* [Dick, the boy] *the story of the Lone Ranger. And we did the segues between the middle of the fifteen chapters. They released it on the big screen as* Hi-Yo, Silver. *With this you see the whole fifteen chapters of The* Lone Ranger *and it's barely an hour. There's less repeating of the previous chapter. Half a page of script catches you up – "meanwhile, back at the ranch."*

> *By the time of The* Range Rider, *Raymond Hatton was an actor rather than doing action. He was getting up there.*

Nasty, vicious Dick Curtis, sometimes nicknamed "the meanest man in Hollywood," was able to lend his brutal villainy to several episodes of *The Range Rider* before his untimely death in 1952 at the age of forty-nine. He had appeared in many Westerns at Columbia. He was one of the developers of Pioneertown, where so many Flying A productions were filmed.

Starting in silents in 1912 and performing until only a few years before his death, Francis McDonald was playing in stock companies before he went before the camera.

He turned to villainy after a panel of editors named him "prettiest man." A leading man in silents, he moved to supporting roles when sound came in. He was one of the villains in *Burn 'Em Up Barnes*, an early serial in which Dick appeared. He worked extensively for Flying A and played sheriffs, henchmen, prospectors and ranchers.

Ed Cobb and Lane Chandler also had been working in Hollywood since the days of silent films. Both could ride and portray a variety of roles. They brought years of experience to the set.

Steve Clark came to film following a twenty-five-year stage career. He came into film at an age to portray fathers, ranchers, an occasional sheriff. He was usually a character in need of help in *The Range Riders*.

One of the newer kids on the block who was handy with action was Boyd "Red" Morgan. He was also handy with dialog and had a good career as a familiar face in almost two hundred films.

Born in Oklahoma, he said he rode horses practically from birth. Before starting in film he played football at USC – which led to him getting a SAG card – then played some pro ball and coached. He saw service in the Navy in World War II.

Dick tells a good story about a gag they did for one of *The Range Rider* episodes.

*On a* Range Rider, *Red Morgan was riding down this trail and I get up on top of a rock and supposedly I'm hidden from his view but actually it's the camera angle. I could see him; he could see me. I'm going to bulldog him off the rock and to make it look more spectacular I like to do a bulldog by diving. I don't jump and land on my feet like a lot of stunt people do.*

*So he says "How you want to do this?"*

*I said, "I'm going to come off the rock and dive behind you and grab you around the shoulders and take you off."*

*He says, "Ok, That sounds good. Don't worry about it. I'll catch you. I won't let you hit the ground."*

*So here he comes. I launch myself, make a perfect dive and caught him on the shoulders and he just kept on riding and I stuck my head in the dirt. Maybe fifteen-sixteen feet down from the top of the rock I came off of and I didn't get a chance to catch him long enough to turn my body around so I didn't stick my head in the dirt.*

*If it had gone right I would have caught him in the shoulders and my weight would have swung my feet around behind him and pulled him off and he would have landed in my lap on the ground. But he just kept on riding and I stuck my nose in the dirt.*

*I said, "How come you didn't come off?"*

*He said, "I didn't feel you."*

*I said, "You didn't?"*

*He said, "No, you got to let me know you're there."*

*I said, "OK, let's do it again."*

*This time I dove in front of him and caught him smack dab in the chest and just rode him all the way down to the ground.*

*He got up and said, "Now I felt you that time."*

Big, hulking Mickey Simpson was a familiar figure for Flying A and was also part of John Ford's company of players. His size made him the perfect henchman to carry out the gang leader's nefarious plans. He menaced the Range Rider and Dick often but never quite got the upper hand.

Dick's voice held rueful humor when he talked about Simpson.

*Mickey Simpson was the most clumsy person that ever was. You'd take your life in your hands doing a fight scene with Mickey Simpson. He'd stumble into you and instead of missing you by four or five inches he'd drive it right through your ears. He was tough to work with [in fights]. Big, clumsy. Very unhandy.*

*I liked him a lot.*

In spite of Dick's evaluation, Simpson becomes downright graceful in the choreography for his fight with Jocko in the episode, "Law of the Frontier." The bartender has a drink with a mickey in it set up on the bar to knockout the judge. When the Range Rider, masquerading as the judge, punches Neil Allen

(Simpson) hard, Allen grabs the drink and chugs it down, getting the knockout potion. When Mickey gets the mickey, his motions become slow motion as Jocko, with a huge grin on his face, sidesteps his punches until the baddie floats slowly down into a chair then onto the floor.

Earle Hodgins was a versatile seasoned character actor with thirty-plus years of stage experience. On *The Range Rider* he played old codger-type roles. Perhaps his portrayal of Shakespearian company owner, Henry Irving Pettigew, in "Romeo Goes West," is the most entertaining.

Younger but still dependable, seasoned and regularly seen on *The Range Rider* were Marshall Reed, Robert J. Wilke (credited as Bob), Jim Bannon, Sheb Wooley and William Haade.

Reed, who kept a side job as a horse trainer, had been a staple in 1940s B-Westerns.

Wilke would get his big break in *High Noon*, though he had done film work for years before its release. He had done some stunting before settling in for a long career as a villain.

Jim Bannon was one of the Red Ryders of film, had done radio work as an actor, announcer and sportscaster and did some stunting. His smooth, distinctive voice was a plus for his many slick villain roles.

Wooley was better known for recording the novelty song hit, "Purple People Eater," than for any acting role, yet he was capable of slick villainy, which he displayed in several episodes of *The Range Rider*.

Haade was the rougher sort of villain. He not only played his share of Western baddies but appeared in a number of crime shows as either the criminal or the cop.

Sam Flint's *Range Rider* appearances were few but it is interesting to note that he shared scenes with young Dickie Jones some fifteen years earlier when Dick portrayed Bobby Mason and Flint played Chief Inspector Henderson in the fifteen-chapter 1937 serial, *Blake of Scotland Yard*.

Though he only appeared in two episodes of *The Range Rider*, it's hard not to give a quick tip of the hat to old familiar face, I.

Stanford "Stan" Jolley. In addition to the Westerns, also worked in stock, vaudeville, radio, on Broadway and even was part of his father's circus and carnival during his childhood. That's experienced!

Several actors whose faces are better associated with regular roles in other series dropped in for a couple of shows – in other words, one week of work.

John Hamilton stopped editing for Clark Kent on *Superman*; Clayton Moore took off his Lone Ranger mask; and Harry Harvey (the sheriff on Roy Rogers' television show) brought his badge over from Mineral City to enforce the law. And before he was hired as Deputy Lofty Craig in the town of Diablo (*Annie Oakley*), Brad Johnson tried unsuccessfully to outwit the Range Rider and Dick.

Dick said he had never worked with Harry Cheshire until *Buffalo Bill, Jr.* but he meant until *The Range Rider*. Cheshire played Judge Ben "Fair and Square" Wiley, the kids' adopted uncle, on *Buffalo Bill, Jr.*, but he also played Dick's uncle in the "Marked Bullets" episode of *The Range Rider*. He had less prominent roles in other episodes.

On the distaff side, few ladies made more than two appearances on *The Range Rider*, but there were a few exceptions.

Lois Hall had a long career stretching from the late 1940s into the first years of the twenty-first century, playing a variety of roles across genres.

She appeared in several episodes and loved it. *In Feature Players, Volume 2*, page 194 (1992), she was quoted:

> *I loved those. . . . I think I enjoyed working* The Range Riders *more than any of the others. I loved Dickie and Jocko and the stunt men there. I love watching stunts. I have the most admiration for the skills they have.*

She added that when her knees were so swollen that she couldn't walk, stuntman Red Morgan carried her all over the set.

Dick remembered her laugh. "Lois Hall had an infectious laugh. She'd break out in a laugh and everybody else would laugh."

She has several notable scenes, one in "Gold Fever." While the Range Rider and Dick are fighting the male villains, she goes after the gang leader, Louise Lorimer, and subdues her.

Only one other woman made as many Range Rider appearances as Lois Hall. That was Elaine Riley. The Ohio beauty was signed by RKO in 1943 and appeared in a variety of films – often in a small role as eye candy. She moved into Westerns and made films with Tim Holt and William "Hopalong Cassidy" Boyd. In the mid-forties she married actor Richard Martin who played sidekick to Tim Holt. She worked on a number of early-fifties television Westerns, including Flying A shows.

Close behind Hall and Riley in appearances was Gloria Saunders, also billed Sanders. Any script that called for a pretty Indian maiden for Dick to sigh over had Saunders on the cast list. She also played the daughter of the Mexican silversmith in "Saga of Silver Town."

Most of the female characters who appeared on *The Range Rider* sent Dick into raptures. Each one was "different," not like the last one who did him dirt or from whom the Range Rider dragged him away.

However, Minerva Urecal was one tough old lady. Dick might admire her toughness but didn't fall in love. After radio and stage work she moved to film at thirty-nine years old and had a good career playing feisty women who annoyed everyone they met.

In *The Range Riders,* she was less annoying and more entertaining because her characters were in the right and she needed help from the Range Rider and Dick.

Before she took on the role of Sky King's niece, Penny, Gloria Winters performed in a few *Range Rider* episodes. She was a daughter in distress more often than a charmer for Dick, but always in need of help.

Margaret Field appeared in four episodes of *The Range Rider* before she took on the role of Jock Mahoney's wife and began using the stage name, Maggie Mahoney. Pretty and petite, her characters infatuated Dick West, unless they became teasingly aggressive, as in "Right of Way."

Other actresses who appeared in *The Range Rider* usually were there for two episodes, one week of work. Among those who enchanted and/or betrayed Dick West were Pamela Blake, Nan Leslie, Gail Davis, Barbara Stanley, Patricia Michon, Donna Martell, Regina Gleason, Gloria Eaton, Wendy Waldron, Gloria Talbot, Karen Sharpe and Kathleen Case.

One other young actress deserves a mention, Sherry Jackson. Dick was asked about working with child actors – and a number of *The Range Riders* had children in them – and he replied:

> *I worked in films as a child and as I got older I worked with child actors. They had a job to do and if they did it, fine, and if they didn't, the director would correct them and they'd do it again.*

> *There was one little girl that blew me away. She was terrific. Boy! She was a good little actress – Sherry Jackson. She was real good. Cute little girl. She was much older than her age. Sherry was great. We worked with a bunch of little girls and she was the top dog.*

Most of the Flying A regulars worked on at least one *Range Rider* but a few came late to the company. Three who did not appear on *The Range Rider* were often seen on *Buffalo Bill, Jr.* – Walter Reed, Lane Bradford and William "Bill" Henry.

Walter Reed appeared as a child in Richard Dix's 1929 film, *Redskins*, but did not seriously start his film career until after serving in World War II. He had performed on stage and made a few films before the war but in the late forties he began to be known as a solid performer, capable of developing good characters.

Dick liked him and commented:

> *People either could ride a horse and do action or they couldn't.*

> *For example: Walter Reed – good actor – worked on a lot of* Buffalo Bill, Jrs. *and* Annie Oakleys. *He worked a lot for Gene Autry.*

> *He says, "Damn! You guys come running out of the barn, you jump on your horses and you're gone and I'm just getting to the hitching post. What's difference here?"*

> *I said, "Walter, you're an actor. Nuff said."*

> *So he calmed down and didn't lose his temper about it.*

> *He said, "Okay, I'm an actor. When I walk out the door, you stunt guys take over."*

*I said, "That's the way to do it."*

*Nice guy.*

Lane Bradford was a second generation baddie. His father, John Merton, menaced many a B-Western hero of the thirties and forties. Bradford started as an extra, a riding extra and doing stunts. As he developed as an actor, he turned over the stunt work to stuntmen. On *Buffalo Bill, Jr.* he regularly threatened Judge Wiley and his adopted children.

William "Bill" Henry was an athlete and a swimmer when young. He started performing in juvenile roles in the thirties. One of his early roles was Gilbert Wynant in *The Thin Man* with William Powell and Myrna Loy. For his television Western roles he was billed as Bill Henry. Dick remembered him as an actor rather than an action person.

A number of background extras – uncredited, often standing around in the background – were handy with some action work. The few times they had a line, the character usually had no name but "henchman." Some of these who probably appeared in more Flying A productions than many of the named performers were Herman Hack, Whitey Hughes, Tex Palmer, Ray Jones, Art Dillard and Frankie Marvin.

# *The Range Rider*

Gene Autry was a fine businessman who saw the possibilities of television quickly. He formed the Flying A production company, which soon was making thirty-minute Western shows aimed at the audience that once filled the theaters for Saturday matinees.

With action a vital aspect, *The Range Rider* was developed. Dick mentioned that Gene held brainstorming sessions for his production people. One of those came up with that most action-filled show of the kiddie Westerns.

Jock Mahoney was tapped for the title role. Jock, who at that time was using the stage name Jack Mahoney, began stunt work in 1946. He was long and lithe and was considered by many to be the finest big stuntman of his time. He was the perfect – perhaps the only – choice for the buckskin-clad hero who might be called the first "man with no name."

Pairing Dick Jones with Jock Mahoney for the show was a stroke of genius. Both men were fine horseman and capable of creating thrilling action sequences. As it turned out, they became a superb team, working well together.

In an interview in 1987, when they appeared together at the Memphis Film Festival, each praised the other for the marvelous shared work experience. Below is a segment of their mutual praise.

*Partners Jock Mahoney and Dick Jones pose for a publicity still for* The Range Rider.

Jocko: *I will truthfully say that working with the young man next to me is probably one of the nicest things that ever happened to me in forty years in the business.*

Fred Davis, film fan and historian, who represented the Memphis Film Festival, contributed the tidbit that Gene Autry developed *The Range Rider* to showcase Jock's talents.

Jocko gave Dick his due: *"This kid was behind me all the time. He did it all, too. All of his own fights, all of his own transfers, all of his own falls. He didn't let me go anyplace, do anything that he wasn't right there at my elbow, at my shoulder, behind me, bringing up the rear, which was his job. As a matter of fact we started – how many days were you out of the hospital after your appendectomy?*

Dick: *It was three or five days. Something like that.*

Jocko: *That was my gutty partner.*

Dick: *I remember we made this vow so that when we went on the road and met all these little kids and they asked, "Did you do that? Did you do that?" We would do it all ourselves so we wouldn't have to lie to the little kids and say, "yes, we did," when we knew a stuntman did it. From that time, everything was pure honesty and we worked it out between the two of us.*

Jocko: *We had a great working relationship and I was very proud to work with Dick as my partner. When we went on the road why they'd say, "Mr. Mahoney, Mr. Jones, we'll put you on the first floor and put Dickie across the hotel on the top floor."*

*I said, "Why you gonna do that?"*

*And they said, "Well, none of you partners get along."*

*And I said, "That's ridiculous. Dickie and I get along very well together. As a partner, my good friend is one of the best."*

Dick: *In my long career in the business, the years I worked with Jock were the best, the happiest, honest, sincere, pure enjoyment.*

*I have tapes of The Range Rider and I watch those all the time. I had more fun doing that and I just sit there and laugh at 'em now.*

Years after that interview, Dick felt the same. "I love watching those *Range Riders*. They were fun. I enjoy watching them today." Dick described the Dick West role he was offered:

*They wanted me to be a comic. I remember they said, "We want you to be a teenage Gabby Hayes," – with a lot of Pat Buttram's crap mixed in it.*

*I said, "I'm the oldest teenager in Hollywood. I can do that job. Okay, I can do that."*

*And I sure did. I acted like a buffoon. That's what they wanted and that's what I did.*

*I believe that the best comedy is when you're trying to be very sincere. Trying to be right is funnier than if you're trying to be funny. So I did it very earnestly and I'm glad somebody thought it was funny.*

According to Dick, *The Range Rider* began filming in October of 1950.

Shortly before that, Dick had the aforementioned surgery. He said, "I had had surgery a few weeks [days is more accurate] before we started *The Range Rider*. Got a girdle and strapped myself up to hold my guts together." Watching him run in the first few episodes, it is possible to see a margin of difference between his movement so close to surgery and the easy flow of his action sequences after the healing was complete.

In conversation about starting out Dick said:

*Got a good story on the first time we worked.*

*When we first got together I'd never met the man [Jock Mahoney] until the day that we worked. Heard about him. Very first day we worked was at Pioneertown. We were out there at the crack of dawn and I'm sitting on one side of the road on a rock and he's sitting on the other side of the road on another rock.*

*The director says, "Okay, guys, let's go." We came together, motioned us in like two fighters. Bring 'em in here. We walked up, toed the mark.*

*We sort of huddle together around the camera and the director says, "This is what we're going to do." It's a long shot.*

*We say OK.*

*Ready? Let's go. Roll 'em, speed, action.*

*Jocko says his stuff and says, "All right. Let's go," and turns away from the scene and swings up on his horse and phsst he's off.*

*I'm sort of shuffling along and get on my horse and trot on out after him. That scene was over. One shot. Bang and it's gone. Good. Print.*

*In the process of moving to the next scene the camera operator – nice guy – comes over to me and says, "Hey, kid, come here."*

*So I come over to him and he says, "What's the name of this show?"*

*I said, "The Range Rider."*

*He said, "Are you the Range Rider?"*

*I said, "No. That tall drink of water is."*

*He said, "Well, let me tell you something. I'm the camera operator and my job is to keep the main man in the center of this viewfinder so he's in center screen all the way through it. I stay on him come hell or high water, not some tag-along. If you want to be in this picture you better whip up and get in his hip pocket."*

*I thought about that for the longest time and couldn't figure out why he was saying that and then I caught on that it's a little screen and they didn't have wide screen at that time and couldn't afford it anyway, so if I'm going to be in it I've got to be right in his hip pocket. I wasn't even in that shot.*

*So I would do everything I could to stay up with him. He'd take one step and I'm two steps behind. I did my best to stay with him without being obvious. He was always swinging up on his horse and gone before he got set in the saddle so I thought okay, I can't get on my horse that quickly because I've got to wait until he goes in front of me so I've got to have my horse running when his horse is running. I'll just do a pony express mount. So I did a lot of them in The Range Rider shows.*

*I did that several times and Jocko never said anything about it and the director never said anything, always a "cut!"*

*I asked the cameraman, "Did you get that?" and he said, "Right in his hip pocket."*

To be accurate, in the final cuts Dick did more pony express mounts in *Buffalo Bill, Jr.* than in *The Range Rider*. Many times it looks as if he were having to restrain his horse to keep from racing ahead of Jocko.

Dick had more than a few comments about the horses he was given to ride in the show.

*Dick rearing Stormy*

*I didn't like the horses they gave me on* The Range Rider *except that last one, the rearing horse.*

*I used five horses for Dick West. The last one that I got was Stormy. He was good at just about everything. I could trick ride off of him.*

*He was a rearing horse. He would stand still for dialog and would let me jump on him from any angle. He turned out to be a real good horse. He's the one I got the rearing shot on.*

*I had to have two chase horses because they were horses that did nothing but run. A couple of chase horses were squirrelly, they were dove hunters. They'd look at anything else except where they were supposed to be going. I couldn't turn them. It took a forty-acre pasture to turn them when they were running. One time I thought I was out like an outrider on a motorcycle trying to keep the thing balanced. One was so skinny you couldn't run him more than twenty-five yards before he'd fall down panting.*

*I had a lot of spotted horses.*

*One thing that dries me to a cinder – the horses they had for me to ride – not one was even close to another* [in markings]. *There were no matching colors or markings. They'd switch them back and forth in the same scene about four times. That would just drive me up a wall.*

*I had no control over the lack of continuity with the paint horses as the scenes changed in* The Range Rider. *That was Gene's idea.*

Many stock long shots were made to insert whenever the Range Rider and Dick took off for the next place or to chase someone. When these were edited together, Dick's horse did indeed swap back and forth. In a segment of less than a minute, Dick would be shown riding three different horses.

The horses were not the only things that changed. The setting did, too, so that they rode through vastly different terrain to go only a short distance. It's the kind of thing critics lambast and devoted fans acknowledge and accept with a tolerant smile.

Dick was not fond of the opening titles to the show.

*In the opening to* The Range Rider *where Jocko swings up on his horse and then transfers to the stagecoach then there's the, "Dick West, All-American Boy," and I'm loping along on the spotted horse and I go over the side and come up under his neck and fire into the camera. That to me is so corny.*

*Watching that thing just burns me. But they wouldn't give me the stuff I asked for in order to get it done the way I did it in* Rocky

Mountain. *I see that thing* [gag from *Rocky Mountain* (1950)] *in half a dozen shows.*

*But this dumb thing on* The Range Rider, *they had this, "you're our bread and butter, if you get hurt, blah, blah, blah," that kind of stuff.*

*So they said, "You can't go any faster than this camera car can go."*

*I said, "You tell the horse that because I have no control over his speed once I get over on the side."*

*Anyway, I think they gave the horse a tranquilizer shot. The horse just loped along like a lazy old plow horse and it looks corny.*

*I fast forward through that. The minute it goes, "dum-dum-dum-dum,* The Range Rider." *I fast forward to get to the story because I don't want to see that dumb thing again.*

Costumes for *The Range Rider* were basic. The Range Rider wore buckskins with plenty of fringe. He did all that action in moccasins rather than supportive footwear. Dick West wore a dark blue shirt with a bib front and jeans with boots. Both often wore gloves, something Dick pointed out was a safety detail, not just for style.

*We actually broke glass in certain scenes. A lot of knickknacks got broken. You could never get all the glass shards up. And there were splinters from broken furniture, stuff like that.*

*Our gloves fit like second skin. You might notice every now and then I'll have mine stuck in my belt. When we were working outside or with the horses it's better to put them on and leave them on. If you forget about them and start to do a gag and stick your hands in the dirt you come up with a bunch of glass slivers.*

*They were bought, not custom-made, but they were real good. The best ones were made out of elk hide — soft. The second best were deerskin. They were small and hard to get on the first time so they fit real good.*

Dick went on to discuss details of his belts.

*The* Range Rider *gunbelt was black leather with the silver conchos on it and the* Buffalo Bill, Jr. *one was brown — light brown. It was the exact same belt in brown.*

*A favorite publicity still that shows the costumes*

There are two things that are noticeable on the belt that holds my pants up. On the right-hand side I've got Rodeo Cowboys Association pin. It's the one Casey Tibbs gave me back in Madison Square Garden when he was World Champion because I had to join the Rodeo Cowboys Association to do that show. He said, "Here's your first pin."

*I had that in the right side of my belt and Gene Autry says, "You're off balance. You've got one pin on one side and nothing on the other side. Add the Turtle Association pin from when you first came here in 1935. So I've got the Cowboy Turtle Association pin on the left side of my buckle and Rodeo Cowboys Association pin on the right.*

Dick never understood his fans' interest in the pieces of memorabilia, damaged or not.

*I've got one or two of them [the* Dick West *shirts] in the trunk in the garage. Don't know if they've been eaten up by moths or not.*

*I know Boyd Magers paid $75 for one that was all ripped up and torn that I threw away at one of the rodeos. He's got it in his memorabilia collection.*

*I told him, "I would've sold you a brand new one for $75."*

In all probability fans would rather have the worn one.

Tricks of the trade and pet peeves were among the things Dick shared in interviews.

*I never had any problem* [with balancing on top of a moving stagecoach]. *A lot of people get seasick just riding on those stagecoaches. It's not the worse thing in the world for stunt people but you've got to make it look good.*

*What I notice more than anything is all the shots they throw at the stagecoach going away. You've got a posse chasing; you've got six or seven guys shooting. They've got those modern Western guns – eighteen-shooters – and they just bang, bang, bang, bang and maybe one guy will get hit, fall off his horse.*

*Guns that never run out of bullets I call eighteen-shooters.*

*They ask, "How come eighteen?"*

*I say, "Well, we use a blank shell called a three-in-one, so three times six is eighteen. So they're eighteen shooters."*

*It satisfies the little kids. They think that's a plausible explanation why they shoot so many times. Three shots out of one hole.*

*I was upstaging Jocko. I couldn't believe the stuff I was getting away with, with him being the star. It finally dawned on me that*

*I was showing off but I was doing it to keep myself in the picture.*

*One of my pet peeves was if I was doing some dialog and have someone right in the camera doing something right behind my shoulder – like they'll take the gun out and open up the gate and see how many slugs, one click at a time. That is very disconcerting. Or walk over to the back wall while the dialog is going on and take a rifle and start examining it and aiming it and all this stuff in the background.*

*If the director doesn't catch it, he's not going to cut. The actor doesn't know what's going on behind him.*

*In scenes I see myself doing this and Jocko's just talking away and I have no idea what he said but I'm really working in the background upstaging him something terrible. I don't know how I got away with it.*

*There's a secret to keeping your hat on in a chase. You dry the hatband off real well and then you wipe the perspiration off and then you lick the front of the hatband and put it down on your forehead with no hairs in the way and it won't come off. The spit and the leather hatband around your head seal.*

*If you turn around and the wind's behind you, it'll probably get under the brim and flip it off the back side but going forward, if you have a nice block and a crease in the hat, it will streamline itself and keep it down.*

He ended that conversation with a joke.

*You know why a cowboy's hat is curled up on the sides of the brim?*

*So they can sit three abreast in a pick-up truck without having to take their hats off.*

Although Dick enjoyed watching these old shows, he couldn't keep from criticizing certain aspects. None of these was obvious to fans unless they watched the shows again and again, but they bothered Dick.

*There was a lot of stock footage in both* Buffalo Bill, Jrs. *and* The Range Riders. *The first thing that you notice is it's not as good a quality as what you're watching. That old stuff looks old.*

*One thing I noticed as I'm watching so many of them is that I keep seeing certain shots that are stock shots. They'll switch the negative on it and make you ride one way, then ride the other direction without ever getting off the horse or turning around. I can always tell because I never have the rope on my left side of the saddle and I never wear my gun on the left side unless I'm doing a part that calls for it. I always wear my gun on the right-hand side with a right-hand holster and they turn me around and run me the other direction and I've got the gun on the other side.*

*You can tell. I'd be riding and I'd have on a right-sided holster and the next time it would be left-handed depending on which way they turned the negative, which way they wanted me to go.*

*There's one [stock shot] that I come hell bent for election into town to go to the sheriff's office. I come chasing into town, do a running dismount and try to outrun the horse to get into the sheriff's office. I always slip at the same spot. Sliding around the corner like that I couldn't believe that I didn't fall down.*

This footage is seen in both "Marked for Death" and "Trail of the Lawless."

Several of these "stock shots" that Dick noticed become obvious to someone who has watched these shows enough to speak the lines with the actors. Most will be noted with the discussion of the individual episodes. A few trends that run through the series follow.

The first shows filmed had features that were modified or eliminated as filming continued.

At the end of the early episodes, the Range Rider and Dick were often thanked before turning and riding off into the sunset in the manner of the Lone Ranger, the Cisco Kid and a number of B-Western heroes. In some, as they leave town, the Range Rider and Dick pass a big saguaro cactus, either the same or similar to the familiar one at the end of the Cisco Kid television shows, and wave goodbye.

Also the formatting of the end titles is different. Earlier crediting ran:

Jack Mahoney
as The Range Rider
Dick Jones
as Dick West.

*A publicity still of the Range Rider and Dick West getting ready to ride away after saving the day.*

Later ones ran:

Jack Mahoney
as
The Range Rider
Dick Jones
as
Dick West.

*Front cover of a well-read issue #6 of* The Flying A's Range Rider *comic book signed by Jock Mahoney*

Armand Schaefer's crediting was also positioned differently.

Early in the series, Range Rider was often called just "Rider," by Dick and others. It is rare to hear this in the second and third seasons.

Certain music riffs used in the first episodes were abandoned as the series moved on.

Dick West was a teenager, ever infatuated by a pretty girl. No matter how many he left behind, for whatever reason – including having his inamorata turn out to be part of the outlaw gang – the next one he fell for was "different." His steady defense line to the Range Rider, when his partner shook his head over Dickie's new love, was, "Oh, but she's different."

However, he was a sweet, naïve kid. All it took to lay him out in a faint was for the girl to grab him and kiss him. His interactions with the girls were part of the humor in the series.

Because Dick West was still an impressionable teenager, the Range Rider worked to teach him skills for living on the range. Sometimes those lessons were an incidental to give the principals an activity to be interrupted when the action began, but in a few episodes the lessons were pertinent to the storyline.

Whenever Dick was called upon to use an alias, his own name was usually used. He became Dick Jones, Richard Jones, Richard P. Jones, Hardrock Jones. His most flamboyant false name was Wildcat Wilson.

Another stock shot is a prison break, used at first of "Treasure of Santa Dolores" and "Gunman's Game." This looks like general stock, not footage shot for *The Range Rider* series.

Many of the images of the Range Rider used in the front titles are used multiple times throughout the series' run. The Range Rider stopping the runaway stage with a small driver supposed to be a woman was probably shot for "Stage to Rainbow's End," in which the woman supposedly driving was Eve Miller. It was used again in the later episode, "Shotgun Stage," in which Elaine Riley was the purported driver.

The Range Rider spawned a series of comic books, as did many of the television shows of the 1950s. Dell released twenty-four issues with Jock Mahoney's picture on the cover. None used a picture of both Dick and Jocko.

# The *Range Rider* Episodes

*The Range Rider* ran for seventy-eight episodes – a three-season run. Autry chose to stop it there. That was the duration to which he had committed. The series was more popular than he had expected and probably could have run for another two or more years but he ended production at the end of the specified term.

In talking of episodes of *The Range Rider*, Dick said, "They all stood on their own."

He continued:

*We'd do two* [Range Riders] *and didn't bother changing scripts. We'd go from one page to the next and change costumes.*

*It's hard for me to remember the chronology of the* Range Riders. *I didn't read the script. I didn't have to. What I wanted to know was, what do I do now? We talked about the gag, rigged up the gag and did it but I don't remember the why and what the routine was and who was there. I just knew they wanted me to be a teenage Gabby Hayes with a lot of Pat Buttram's gags thrown in and I said, "Yes. I can do that."*

Action was the name of the game. Every episode contains at least one well-choreographed fight. Most of them have more than one, as well as chase scenes, runaway wagons, saddles falls, bulldogging. Whatever Western action exists, it happened in *The Range*

*Rider* shows. Individual episode fights are discussed if something out of the standard array of action occurred, otherwise finely choreographed fights are understood to be a part of every show.

Because the episodes had no sequence and different listings show them in different order they are listed in alphabetical order with the ones showing a 1950 copyright on the front titles grouped together at the first. The director (D:) and scriptwriters (S:) plus the copyright date are shown for each episode.

# 1950 Episodes

## "The Baron of Broken Bow"
D: John English
S: Elizabeth Beecher
© 1950

Dick is riding into Cedar Valley on the stage, on top with the driver, when they see two rowdies harassing a wagon with a man, Soapy Lester (Hal K. Dawson), and a girl, Cindy Gordon (Patricia Michon), in it. Dick insists that they interfere, against the stage driver's wishes.

The Range Rider rides up in time to help run off the baddies. He and Dick pretend not to know each other. Dick introduces himself as Dick Jones from Chicago.

Cindy tells them that Lance West (Leonard Penn), the Baron of Broken Bow, is running them out of the valley. He's a cattleman and they raise sheep. [Penn also plays Dick's father in "The Range Rider," but there he is a gambler called Rivers.]

Soapy suddenly says he's decided not to run. He's staying. The Range Rider suggests that Cindy do the same. Doc Tomlin (Tom London) would probably put her up.

The Doc says she can stay as long as she wants. He tells the Range Rider that the baron is out for blood. West believes the sheepmen are rustling his cattle. Soapy says that isn't true.

Meanwhile West is chewing out his henchmen for letting the roving strangers get the best of them.

When the stage pulls up and the baron sees Dick, he sends his boys to bring him to the office. Dick is his son. Dick refuses to go with the men and the Range Rider helps him fight them off. West himself comes out to fetch Dick. He and the Range Rider agree to talk and West is forced into a meeting between himself and the sheepmen at a neutral location, the doctor's office.

West's henchmen are troubled. Red Stratton (Don C. Harvey), the baron's foreman, is running his own operation – stealing his boss' cattle and blaming the sheepmen. He moves quickly to protect his arrangement.

At two o'clock, when the peace meeting starts, the henchmen

raid and destroy a sheepman's property and at the same time run cattle off West's range. Cindy rushes into the meeting to report the betrayal, then Stratton rides up to tell West his herd has been hit. The talk goes from peace to war.

The Range Rider knows a third party triggered this and asks to be given until noon the next day to prove it. He and Dick have their work cut out for them.

## "The Crooked Fork"
## D: John English
## S: Paul Gangelin
## © 1950

Two riders come in from different directions. Each dismounts and gets the drop on the other only to discover they are father and daughter, Cheerful Wilson (Raymond Hatton), who has been left in charge of the sheriff's office while the official is sick, and his daughter Ruth (Eve Miller). Both are out looking for the bandits who keep robbing the freight wagons.

They see two strange riders on the horizon, the Range Rider and Dick. Cheerful arrests them while they are still trying to make sense of his accusations. He sends Ruth to tell Bert that the robbers are in custody and it is safe to go ahead.

The bandits watch Ruth deliver the message and as soon as she leaves ride down and attack the wagon. The Range Rider, Dick and Cheerful hear the shots and Range Rider manages to convince Cheerful to let them help.

Back in Crooked Fork, Cheerful and Ruth tell the about the problems they are having getting the freight through. Range Rider asks if the line turns a big profit and Ruth says often they barely make ends meet. He responds that there must be a hidden reason for these attacks.

Wayne Cooper (Jim Bannon) comes in and demands action against the robbers from Cheerful, as he was left in charge. He adds that the town wants him to resign. No one will continue to use his freight line. Cooper is starting a freight service with his wagon, which he will protect. The Range Rider wants to know why he can't protect Cheerful's wagon. Cooper retorts that Cheerful

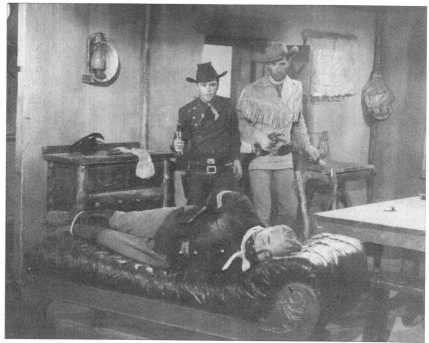

*Dick West and the Range Rider find the Army messenger (Kenne Duncan) tied up in the outlaws' cabin.*

has a history of blunders.

After he leaves, the Range Rider asks why Cooper wants Cheerful's business. Cheerful has no idea.

Cooper goes to his henchmen and tells them not to raid Cheerful's wagon today. He has another job for them. An Army messenger will be riding through. Cooper wants the information he carries kept secret until he owns Cheerful's equipment. He tells his boys to capture him and keep him out of circulation for a few days.

As they wrestle with him, he fires his gun. The Range Rider and Dick, riding guard on Cheerful's wagon, hear it and ride to check it out. The Range Rider finds a button from an Army uniform. That and other clues will help him deduce the reason for Cooper's underhanded dealings and put Cheerful back in the freight business.

"The Range Rider"
D: George Archainbaud
S: Lawrence Hazard
© 1950

If this episode was not the pilot script, it was certainly written
to set up the premise of the series. It is also the only episode sum-
marized here to the final scene.

Two bandits wearing fake bushy beards hide in the rocks watching the road. First they see the Range Rider coming down the trail.
Then they see John "Paleface" Rivers (Leonard Penn), a gambler
from Whetstone, pulling brush across the path.

When the Range Rider reaches the brush pile, Rivers holds him
up to take his horse. The gambler mounts Rawhide but the horse
throws him and now Range Rider is in charge. He walks Rivers
back to Whetstone.

In the town hotel Dick is watching from a window as the Range
Rider brings Paleface in. His Aunt Jennie (Anne Nagel) tells him
that staring out the window isn't helping her pack. He stalls her off
to watch the action on the street.

The Range Rider stops Rivers in front of Sheriff Jim McCoy
(Kenneth MacDonald), who tells the gambler he just doesn't seem
to have any luck at all. Paleface grabs the sheriff's gun and says he
isn't going back to jail.

Dick runs from the window for a rifle to stop the gambler but his
aunt holds him back. She tells him the gambler is his father.

The Range Rider kicks the gun from Rivers hand. Dick watches
the fight from the window as Paleface snatches the gun from the
ground but then throws it aside without using it.

The sheriff turns him loose with a "get out of town" and tells the
Range Rider he must not be much of a sheriff. He hates to lock
them up if they have a spark of good in them.

He also gives Rider the background on Rivers. The gambler had
a table in the saloon until Hannigan (Bill Kennedy), the express
agent, claimed he was bottom dealing. No proof, but Rivers was
told to leave town.

When the sheriff gets to introductions, the Range Rider says,
"Just call me Rider." McCoy knows he means the Range Rider and

asks him to come by after he eats. He also asks him to tell Hannigan to come to his office.

In the hotel, Dick's aunt tells him that his father spent years in prison for killing a man in defense of Dick's mother. Dick now wants to catch up with the man he has never really known but who is his father.

Meanwhile, Hannigan and the sheriff are puzzling over how the bearded bandits know when there is money in transit. Someone must be tipping them off. Ten thousand dollars will be going out today but the sheriff plans to send it by the Range Rider and put an empty money box on the stage.

Dick overhears the conversation and tells his aunt it's a good thing they are honest. He knows the Range Rider will be carrying the money to Hellgate, sixty miles across the desert.

As the Range Rider gets ready to leave, he and the sheriff see the express agent riding out of town. McCoy tells Range Rider if he sees the bearded bandits at the half-way point or at Thompson's he might pick them up. They have prices on their heads.

Down the road two bearded bandits watch the stage go by. They have no tip. It must not have money on it. Then Hannigan rides up and tells them the Range Rider is carrying the money. One of the bandits resists tangling with him.

Hannigan is scornful. "Two of you and one of him."

"But he's dynamite," they protest, yet reluctantly head for the half-way point. The boss goes to get the rest of the gang and head for Thompson's.

The henchmen are right. The Range Rider gets the best of them and takes them along as prisoners as they push on to Thompson's

There Dick and his father are discussing taking the money from Range Rider. Dick knows it is wrong. His mother impressed that on him until her dying day. His dad agrees but says circumstances are such that "just this once" he feels it's the only way.

Hannigan and the rest of the gang are watching from the rocks. The Range Rider knows this when he and his prisoners reach Thompson's. He uses the horses and the bearded bandits to get into the shack without giving the baddies an open target, but Dick's father is waiting behind the door when he walks in. Rider spins and gets the drop on him but Dick turns the tables by holding a rifle on the Range Rider.

Paleface is patting him down hunting the money when Dick stops him. He can't steal for any reason. It's wrong.

Rivers grabs the gun, pushes his son aside and ties up the Range Rider. Rider cautions him about the gang outside but he and Jennie go out to hitch up the horses.

While they are outside Dick and the Range Rider talk about right and wrong. Dick asks Rider bluntly if he would side with a stranger who is in the right against his own father. The Range Rider hesitates, then shamefacedly tells Dick no. Then Dick realizes that the Range Rider is being totally honest with him.

The bearded bandits attack and Dick's father and aunt rush back in. Rivers turns the Range Rider loose to help and one of his prisoners, Gansby (Gregg Barton) offers to help, too.

He swaps clothes with the Range Rider and, as the sun sets, the Range Rider, in Gansby's clothes and bushy beard, runs from the cabin as if he is escaping. He drops, pretending he has been shot. Hannigan and the gang rush toward him and that's the end of them. He unmasks Hannigan as the connection between money shipment schedules and the robbers.

They all ride together to the junction. The Range Rider leaves them there to make the final entry into Hellgate without him.

But Dick wants to know him better. When his aunt remarks that no one thanked Rider, Dick says he'll give him everyone's thanks and goes after the Range Rider to be his partner.

In "The Range Rider," Kenneth MacDonald plays Sheriff Jim McCoy. [Was someone's mind thinking Tim McCoy?] His character is one of the most richly developed of all the supporting roles in the series. He has some of the most entertaining lines and the old pro plays the character to the hilt. It's worth watching this episode just to see him.

## "The Secret Lode"
## D: George Archainbaud
## S: Kenneth Perkins
## © 1950

This early episode opens with baddies hearing that the Pudies have sent for the Range Rider to help them. The outlaws plan to attack before he reaches the area.

Billy (Tommy Ivo) is outside catching lizards when he sees riders coming and runs in to tell his parents (Leonard Penn and Anne Nagel), who are hiding their gold under bricks around the fireplace. Pa and Uncle Ben (Harry Cheshire) break out the guns. Ma unreasonably blames the Range Rider because he hasn't arrived yet. Pa is wounded and as soon as all the gold is hidden, they wave a white dishcloth from the door.

The Range Rider and Dick West ride up as the bandits are walking to the house and run them off.

The Range Rider and Uncle Ben go out and see an Apache, who dashes away when they see him. Rider gives chase but tells Unk not to mention the Indian to the family. No point in adding to their anxiety.

While he is gone the robbers come back. When Pa won't tell where the gold is, they kidnap Billy.

Ma immediately declares the Range Rider has joined the outlaws because he wasn't there when they came back.

The Pudies are so ugly and rude to him, only the Range Rider – or Mother Teresa – would continue to try to help them.

But help them he does – with loads of full-tilt action.

## "Six Gun Party"
## D: George Archainbaud
## S: Samuel Newman
## © 1950

The Range Rider and Dick West see a woman, Sharon Miller (Elaine Riley), lying in wait in the rocks with a rifle to bushwhack someone.

She's waiting for Barney Kimball (Denver Pyle), who is trying to take the ranch from her and her uncle, John "Whiskers"

*Top: Crew filming the Range Rider and Dick West inspecting ground sign. Bottom: Close up of the same scene.*

Miller (Earle Hodgins), just as he has done to others throughout the basin.

Kimball thinks Sharon has hired the Range Rider to help her and knocks him in the head with a gun while he fights with Max (Dick Curtis), who then kicks him around. The Range Rider is battered and, after the attackers ride off, they take him to Sharon's ranch to patch him up.

When he comes to and asks where Dick is, Whiskers tells him, "He went for a ride."

Sharon and her uncle fill the Range Rider in on the events that have taken place and then Sharon mentions that Dick asked the whereabouts of Kimball's ranch before he left.

The three of them ride out to rescue Dick, who does need rescue. He is caught and slapped around but the villains talk in front of him. Now he knows their plans for tonight.

It may not be necessary to know what they are planning for the Range Rider has plans of his own, which include taking every precaution to remove the guards as they move in on Kimball's ranch.

The hallmark of this series was action and there's plenty of it before right wins out.

## "Stage to Rainbow's End"
## D: John English
## S: Paul Gangelin
## © 1950

Jack Keenan (Jim Bannon) sends his boys down to attack the stage and bring the passenger to him. He takes the man's papers and kills him.

The Range Rider and Dick stop the stage horses as they lope along on their own and find the dead driver. They backtrack the path and come to the site of the holdup where the ground sign shows that four riders took a passenger from the stage with them. At the end of the tracks leading from the stage they find the dead passenger with no papers or identification on him. The only thing still in his clothes is a miniature locomotive.

Rainbow's End is the closest town so they take the stage and the dead man there.

In town, Dry Gulch (Raymond Hatton) sees the stage coming and calls Amy (Eve Miller). She turns away crying when she sees the dead driver, who was her Uncle Dave (Boyd Stockman).

Keenan is watching from across the street. He walks over and introduces himself, telling the Range Rider he is part owner of the stage line.

Inside the stage office Amy tells the Range Rider there is no reason for the stages to be attacked. They carry few passengers and little freight. Sometimes the only reason for a run is to keep the franchise. The town is dying.

While the Range Rider is getting information from Amy and Dry Gulch, Dick is in the saloon spouting braggadocio about the Range Rider. Why Rider can do it all – shoot, track, fight. He can beat two men single-handed.

After Dick leaves, Keenan taunts Rusty (Tom Monroe) and Joe (Bob Woodward), saying they looked scared when they heard about the Range Rider. They can't wait to pick a fight by the time Keenan quits talking. They burst into the stage office and jump on the Range Rider. He does beat two men single-handed.

Then he chastises Dick for shooting off his mouth, but he suspects that it took more than Dick's words to get such a rise out of the rowdies. Somebody who doesn't want him and Dick around egged them on.

So, since there seems to be evil afoot and Amy's a pretty nice girl and in trouble, they'll hang around to help her.

To leave Amy without a stage driver, Keenan has his men kidnap Dick. Then he tells the Range Rider that men took Dick away, sending Range Rider out to search for him. They knock out Dry Gulch, leaving him dizzy. With no one else to drive Amy, will do it herself.

Keenan orders his men after the stage but his henchman Mark (Kenne Duncan) protests that he doesn't shoot women. That may slow things down but it will take intervention from the Range Rider and Dick to round up all the villains and discover the meaning of the miniature locomotive.

## 1951-1953 Episodes
## "Ambush at Coyote Canyon"
## D: Ross Lederman
## S: John K. Butler
## © 1952

Al (Harry Lauter) stops the stage to Placerville, shoots Clay Matthews (Judd Holden) and kills the driver. He makes a pass at Joyce Lanyon (Nan Leslie). His boys are ready to get moving but it takes the appearance of the Range Rider and Dick to run them off.

The Range Rider leaves Dick to drive the stage to the Sweetwater stage depot but Joyce says she can drive the stage. "You can drive a four-up?" Dick asks. "I can drive a six-up," she retorts, leaving Dick to go help his partner chase the bandits.

They stop the chase in the rough rocks and go back to Sweetwater to talk to the wounded man. He is a Wells Fargo agent. Though he will heal fine, he has business to do that won't wait, so he asks the Range Rider and Dick for help.

The Eureka Mining Company at Placerville can't get gold through to Sacramento. No matter what efforts are made to keep the plans for shipment secret, the bandits find out. There must be an inside man.

Matthews tells the Range Rider he doesn't care how he manages it, but the gold must get through to Sacramento.

Sheriff Jim Austin (Lane Chandler) and his deputy, Bert Lanyon (Kermit Maynard), are talking with Martin Wickett (Clayton Moore) about protecting the gold that is in the office safe when Joyce comes in to tell them about the holdup. Lanyon stays on guard.

The Range Rider and Dick break in and "steal" the gold by blowing the safe and hiding the loot right there in the office. Joyce comes back with food for her father and sees them through the window.

The next morning they ride into town to report to Wickett that they are working for Wells Fargo and have hidden the gold in the office. Joyce sees them and calls the sheriff to arrest them. When the lawman comes in with gun drawn, Wickett refuses to support them and they end up in jail.

He not only refuses to vouch for them, but tells them he can't wait to ship the gold. It must go out on the noon stage. Now they have a pretty good idea who the inside connection to the outlaws is.

It's up to them to come up with a scheme to get out of the cell in time to save the gold. When Joyce comes in protesting that a "young boy" like Dick is in the same cell with an adult criminal, they are practically out the door.

## "Bad Medicine"
## D: George Archainbaud
## S: Dwight Cummins
## © 1951

The Range Rider and Dick have stopped to rest the horses and are practicing fighting when three outlaws on the run see their horses. Ty Smith (Alan Hale, Jr.) sneaks up to take them but the Range Rider catches him. The two others (Bob Woodward and Marshall Reed) come in guns blazing. The outlaws escape, but not with the horses.

In town the Range Rider and Dick talk with Sheriff Clark (Edgar Dearing), who tells them that the three are probably the same ones who robbed the bank and killed the teller that morning. The sheriff asks for help.

The Range Rider and Dick plan to leave their pack mule at Dick's Uncle Ben's (Francis McDonald). They find the old man badly wounded on the floor and his horses gone. They break from hunting the villains to get Uncle Ben back to town and a doctor.

Dick stays in town with his uncle while the Range Rider and the sheriff get back on the trail. He follows after his uncle dies.

When it comes time for the final trap, Dick and the sheriff will be backing up the Range Rider.

This episode is *very* basic. Only the outlaw leader has a name. There is no girl about whom for Dick to say, "Oh. But she's different." Other than Dick's Uncle Ben, there are three baddies and three pursuers. The screenwriter wrote numerous episodes. The director was seasoned and reliable. There is plenty of good Range Rider action. It's not that this is a bad episode; but it feels like something is missing.

## "Bad Men of Rimrock"
## D: William Berke
## S: Milton Raison
## © 1952

Tom Pinckert (Stanley Andrews) built the town of Rimrock on his homestead. He has rented a place for a casino to Donald Moore (Jim Bannon) but has discovered Moore's games are crooked and his friends are being swindled. Pinckert is throwing Moore out, terminating the deal.

Moore terminates the deal by shooting the old man point blank. The casino owner sends his henchman Bill (Gregg Barton) for the coroner, who is on their payroll. The story that is released is that Pinckert had a heart attack.

Tom leaves all his property to a relative from the East, Leslie. Moore and his boys, Bill and Pete (Mickey Simpson), go to the stage to meet the man they need to fool. The man is a woman, Tom's sister (Minerva Urecal). She has brought her niece, Jane Collins (Gloria Eaton), with her. Her first move is to get a buckboard and drive out to the Pinckert ranch.

Moore tells his men that they will let the women go alone. No telling what might happen along the way, especially when he gives them instructions to attack the buckboard.

The Range Rider and Dick hear the gunshots and rush to give the women a hand. Feisty Leslie tells their rescuers that they'll be fine until she notices Jane and Dick making eyes at each other. Then she agrees to the Range Rider's offer of an escort. She also agrees to letting them stay at the ranch for protection until some questions are answered.

Leslie wants details concerning the way her brother died. She also is puzzled about the attack on them on the road. They all go to town to look for answers. While Jane goes shopping, her aunt goes straight to Don Moore's office. The Range Rider and Dick wait for her outside.

Bill and Pete pick a fight with the Range Rider and Dick. Moore gives Leslie a glib story and says Range Rider and Dick are rowdies. Leslie believes neither Moore's story about her brother's death nor that her new protectors are anything but gentlemen.

In fact, she tells Moore flatly that she will be making some changes. She's more than a match for him. Even threatening notes thrown through her bedroom window don't deter her determination. With the Range Rider and Dick at her back she's a tenacious bulldog resolved to get to the bottom of this matter and clean up the town.

The film was misedited in one scene in this episode. While the Range Rider and Moore are fighting in the office, Leslie holds a gun on Pete with the door behind her closed. In the next view of them, she is closing the door behind her.

## "The Bandit Stallion"
**D: Wallace Fox**
**S: Betty Burbridge**
**© 1952**

In several B-Westerns, dogs were used to kill. In "Bandit Stallion," the thieves are using a stallion to steal horses for them. It makes a puzzle when no tracks of ridden horses can be found around the pen.

The Harris kids, Geri (Gloria Winters) and Tommy (B.G. Norman) are members of the W.F.F. club. Dick worked at the Harris ranch the year before and helped organize the group. The initials stand for work, fun and friendliness. Now the kids are having a show and have invited Dick back to be the judge of their efforts.

As Dick and the Range Rider near the Harris ranch they hear gunshots and gallop to the site. They find Dick's old boss, Mr. Harris (Pierre Watkin), in a gunfight with horse thieves who ran off his mares.

The Range Rider and Dick try to circle around but the robbers escape. However, with neither the horses nor their own mounts.

Harris and his crew round up the horses but Tommy's project colt, Dandy, is missing still.

The bandits walk until one can walk no more and end up trapped in the Harris barn. They hide in the hayloft and settle in. The next morning, every time they try to escape someone else comes into the barn. After all, it is the site of the show.

When the Range Rider goes out to look for Tommy's colt before the show, he finds the tracks of the outlaws leading to the Harris barn. However, catching the thieves must take a back seat to the important business of judging the kids' projects. The theme here is a feel-good one about kids learning responsibility and skills needed for life on a ranch.

In this show the thieves are comic relief. Chubby's (William Haade) hunger is a key to their capture. When he eats the cake Geri made for the show, he gets such a stomach ache that he can't go on. The Range Rider gives Geri an award for helping capture the bandits.

This is an atypical episode. No one is shot, the thief is a horse and fights are few and far between.

## "Big Medicine Man"
## D: Wallace Fox
## S: Dwight Cummins
## © 1951

The Range Rider and Dick are tracking outlaws Trigger Morrison (Denver Pyle) and Matt Green (Duke York) for Wells Fargo. The bandits disappear behind a heavy wooden gate with "Keep Out" signs on it.

When Range Rider and Dick climb over the gate after them, Ed Fallon (Al Bridge) shoots at them. He bought the land six months ago and put up the barrier. The gate blocks off the wash where the Indians get colored sand for their ceremonies and Fallon is prejudiced against Indians. He says no one has come through his gate, but as soon as the Range Rider and Dick leave he goes back to join Trigger and Matt, with whom he is in cahoots.

The Range Rider's blood brother White Eagle (Chief Yowlachie) climbs over the gate next. He is in need of sand for ceremonies to bring rain. Trigger sees him and shoots him.

His daughter Piñon (Sandra Valles) sees the Range Rider and tells him that her father needs help from his blood brother.

The Range Rider finds White Eagle and takes him home but sand is necessary for a healing ceremony. The Range Rider steps up and goes to the wash to gather sand as an Indian.

He is attacked by Matt and Trigger, who think he *is* an Indian.

They are pleased to find out that they have captured the Range Rider.

Fortunately, Dick and Piñon did not stay behind as they were told to do. Help is on the way.

**"The Black Terror"**
**D: Ross Lederman**
**S: William Telaak**
**© 1953**

The Range Rider and Dick stop and look down on the sleepy little town where the Range Rider's friend Jim Walsh (Ewing Mitchell) is sheriff. Gunshots break the silence and the two race to the scene of the incident. They find Irene Danning (Regina Gleason) bending over the body of her father. She tells them a masked man rode up, shot her father and rode away. Range Rider and Dick follow the trail but lose it in the rocks.

The head of the Citizens' Committee, Ed Finley (I. Stanford Jolley), is in the sheriff's office berating Walsh for not catching the man who has recently killed four men in the area, with no obvious motive. Irene is there listening and to report her father's murder.

Until Irene, no one had seen the killer so there was no chance to identify him. The Range Rider borrows a piece of charcoal, clears a place on the office wall and begins sketching as he pulls details of description from Irene as she can remember them.

Then the Range Rider and Dick borrow a dummy from the general store and create the image in 3-D. When the sheriff looks at it, he says if he had not been there for Dan Gannon's execution, he'd know that Gannon is the killer.

The Range Rider and Dick go out to talk to the families of the victims to try to find a common thread. One of the widows tells them her husband was on the jury that convicted Dan Gannon.

On the way home they hear shots and chase a runaway buckboard. The dying man driving it names the man who shot him as Dan Gannon. He was on the jury, too. As they soon learn, so were all the others who were murdered.

It will be tough for the Range Rider to capture and jail a ghost for the killings.

For Smiley Burnette fans, Dick's masquerade as the town barber in this episode will have familiar bits of business. The segment is almost a duplicate of one Smiley played in a Durango Kid film. Familiar face Emil Sitka plays Dick's customer (victim?) in the farcical scene.

## "Blind Canyon"
## D: Wallace Fox
## S: Robert Schaefer and Eric Freiwald
## © 1952

Scotty Tyler (B.G. Norman) and his grandfather (Stanley Blystone) are loading gold from a mine to a wagon when bandits (Marshall Reed, Boyd "Red" Morgan and William Haade) make them go into the mine, then blow up the mine entry and steal the wagon.

The Range Rider and Dick hear the explosion and dash to the scene to find Scotty still alive but his grandfather dead. They take him to Dr. Moore's office in town where the doctor (Frank Jaquet) determines he is blind. The doctor tells Scotty's sister, Linda (Gloria Winters), that he knows of a doctor in San Francisco, a Dr. Chancellor (Pierre Watkin), who may be able to restore Scotty's sight.

The Range Rider and Dick send for Dr. Chancellor and stay around to help Linda get Scotty back on his feet. The doctor thinks he should be active.

When the outlaws hear that Scotty is alive, they go to the ranch to kill him. Upon learning that he is blind they let him live, but they have made the danger obvious.

Upon hearing that a doctor is coming to restore Scotty's sight, they plan to get rid of him, too, but the Range Rider is one step ahead of them and swaps clothes with the doctor to assure his safe passage.

The surgery is successful but the outlaws are still at large. Only Scotty knows what they look like. He will have to identify them before they can be captured, and must hide the fact that he can see again until then.

The Range Rider comes up with a plan to trap the outlaws and give Scotty a clear look at them.

This exact same story, with the change from a blind boy to a blind girl, is used for the *Annie Oakley* episode, "Valley of the Shadows." Even some of the lines are the same. It, too, was written by Robert Schaefer and Eric Freiwald,

## "The Blind Trail"
## D: George Archainbaud
## S: Joe Richardson
## © 1951

This episode begins with humor. The Range Rider calls for a stop to take a nap. Dick is insulted. He's an adult; he doesn't need one. Range Rider wins and gunshots wake them from their sleep.

Two of Starkey's henchmen attack Judy Harper (Lois Hall) on the road. The Range Rider and Dick run them off. After the excitement, Judy feels a little faint so Dick, smitten again, insists on driving her home.

There her father, Jed Harper (John Parrish) explains that Starkey (James Griffith) is the crooked mayor of Sunrise and he, Harper, is running against him. Starkey will do anything to hold on to the office.

Harper's friend Hank Bradley (Tom London) is his chief supporter, though Harper believes Hank is the one who should be mayor.

The Range Rider and Dick ride into town to have a talk with Sharkey. Range Rider goes into the office and leaves Dick on guard outside.

Two of the mayor's men sucker Dick into a barn to trap him but in a slam-bang fight he gets the best of both of them.

Sharkey has to get rid of the Range Rider and Dick. He comes up with a plan to kill *three* birds with one stone. He kills Hank Bradley and frames the Range Rider and Dick for the killing.

The sheriff (Edgar Dearing), also one of Sharkey's men, locks up the Range Rider but the boss tells him to release Dick. He has still another plan.

Dick goes back to the cabin where Bradley was killed and discovers a hidden door in the back wall. He is captured and now has to work his way free to keep his partner from being shot in the fake escape trap Sharkey has set up.

Dick remembered "The Blind Trail" for a gag he thought up.

*That's the one where I was mooning and lollygagging around Lois Hall. "Judy's a beautiful name."*

*I was in the house and Jocko started to leave and he said, "Come on." But I'm still hanging around Judy and he hollers real loud and I go through the window [panel] by the door.*

*That was rigged up between me and the director.*

*I said, "I want to do this because I think this will be funny."*

*I told him about it and he said, "I think it will be, too, so we won't tell anybody. We'll just add some sound effects with no glass in that window."*

*So when Jocko hollers, I just turned and went right through the long window beside the door. Lois didn't know we were going to do it and she broke up and laughed so hard. It was hilarious just to watch her laugh. They left that in the scene.*

*There was no glass in there so I made the script girl make a note to the sound effects man to add a breaking window sound in there. I went through the hole and took the curtain with me but there was no glass in the opening. I thought that was a funny gag.*

## "Border City Affair"
## D: Frank McDonald
## S: Norman S. Hall
## © 1953

The Range Rider and Dick hear shots and ride up to find George Colfax, sheriff of Border City, standing over the body of Sam Blades, whom he has just shot. He asks them to take Blades into Border City to a doctor while he rounds up his posse.

When they get to town, the body hanging over the saddle – he died on the way – is identified as that of Sheriff Colfax. Blades had stolen the sheriff's badge.

Banker Clyde Armstrong (John Doucette) tells them Blades held up the bank that morning and Sheriff Colfax went after him. Armstrong accuses them of being cohorts of Blades.

Curly Bill (Myron Healey) tries to stir up a lynching, but Dick gets the drop on the men. He and the Range Rider dash out of town with the gang of townsmen hot on their heels. As soon as they lose the posse, they double back and hold up in a barn the Range Rider spotted on the edge of town.

Gail Colfax (Jean Willes), the sheriff's niece, gets the drop on them but soon sits down to tell them about Armstrong's shady dealings and her uncle's suspicions. She feels sure that the banker and Sam Blades (Brad Johnson) are connected.

She tells them that Armstrong's ranch is the Quarter-Circle A, and gives them directions to get there. If they need to see her, she lives behind the sheriff's office. The Range Rider and Dick go out to the ranch to investigate.

Blades reports to Armstrong at his ranch. The boss is pleased with the status overall but needs to steal the affidavits the sheriff has been gathering that are still in the safe in his office. It will be easy to get the deputy out of the way but Armstrong himself will need to trick Gail into leaving.

The Range Rider and Dick sneak into Armstrong's house and overhear Curly Bill and Blades talking. Dick trips and the outlaws hear the noise, which is a great opportunity for a knock-down, drag-out, tear-up-the-room fight.

Armstrong takes the money to replace what he has stolen from the bank vault and goes to Gail with a ruse to get her to go with him.

Gail is suspicious and leaves clues for the Range Rider to let him know where she's been taken.

When Range Rider and Dick get to the sheriff's office and find her gone, the Quarter-Circle A's drawn in lipstick send them on the right path to save Gail and round up the baddies.

**"Border Trouble"**
**D: Thomas Carr**
**S: Earle Snell**
**© 1952**

The Range Rider and Dick ride across the border into Canada to check out gunshots. They find a dead trapper. Tracks of two horses lead away from the site so they go in pursuit of the killers. Several

Royal Canadian Mounted Policemen see them ride off, think they are the perpetrators and take off after them. At the border, they stop. Two of the Mounties change out of uniform and follow them across the border to the United States.

Luke (Robert J. Wilke [billed here as Bob]) and Jim (Boyd "Red" Morgan), the real killers, are hiding three albino fox skins in an old barn. Luke plans to tell the boss they must have killed the wrong trapper and sell the albino skins for his personal profit.

To confuse trackers, when they leave the barn they put moccasins with reversed horseshoes attached on their horses hooves.

Range Rider and Dick get to the barn and see only tracks leading to the place. The Mounties follow them to the barn and try to arrest them, but the Range Rider and Dick fight them and get away. They have no way to know their accosters are lawmen from Canada.

Back at the outlaw hideout, the boss is furious when Luke and Jim show up without the pelts. Luke pretends to be sick and stays behind when Jim takes the rest of the gang to the body of the trapper.

The Range Rider and Dick go back to the barn and find Luke getting the skins for his Indian girlfriend Rabbit (Gloria Saunders) and her mother to take to the trading post. Range Rider betters him in a fight and goes to backtrack his horse, leaving Dick behind to tie up Luke and wait for the Range Rider to return.

Rabbit has followed and suckers Dick away, pretending to be on a runaway horse. He is knocked out in a fall. She goes back and frees Luke, who gives her the skins for her mother to take to the trading post.

The Range Rider returns to the barn after searching the outlaw cabin and finds it empty.

Rabbit has taken Dick to the hideout with her. She wants to keep him. When Luke comes in and sees Dick, he wants to kill him. He getting the horses when the Range Rider rides up and knocks Luke out in a fight.

About that time, the rest of the gang return. Now Range Rider, Dick and Rabbit are trapped in the cabin. The Range Rider suggests a ruse to make up for lack of ammunition. There is a cute bit of by-play between Dick and Rabbit. In a change of routine, Dick does *not* fall for her.

The ruse works but it takes a lot of action to wind up this episode and help the Mounties get their fur-smuggling men.

## "The Buckskin"
## D: Frank McDonald
## S: Arthur Rowe
## © 1953

The Range Rider is waiting for Dick when three Army men ride up, Major Clint Ramsey (Steve Darrell), Sergeant Richmond (Paul McGuire) and a private (John Pickard).

Richmond and the Range Rider had wrangled horses together in the past and Richmond has always wanted the Range Rider's buckskin. The major hits Range Rider in the head, knocking him out, and tells Richmond he should always take what he wants. He steals the buckskin.

Dick arrives at the meeting place and brings the Range Rider around. They go to the fort to report the theft.

Range Rider introduces himself and Dick to the colonel (Stanley Andrews), who tells them the real Major Clint Ramsey was ambushed and killed six months ago. The fake major and his men have been robbing homesteaders' wagons in uniform, introducing themselves as soldiers and putting the blame on the Army.

Major Ramsey's grandson Bobby (Peter Votrian) comes in as the Range Rider is explaining his plan to trap the fake soldiers.

Bobby wants to go with them when they masquerade as settlers but the colonel denies permission. Of course, the boy disobeys orders and hides in the wagon, making it much more difficult for the Range Rider and Dick to capture his grandfather's killers.

Difficult or easy they manage to save themselves and Bobby and clear the Army's reputation.

## "Bullets and Badmen"
D: Frank McDonald
S: Edward Llewellyn
© 1953

Outlaw Haley (Brad Johnson) comes into Dr. Collins' office to get help for his partner who had an "accident." The doctor leaves with him.

Pop Begley's (Al Bridge) team brings his wagon in with him wounded. He tells the Range Rider that three men jumped him and took his money belt. The doctor has gone but they get Begley settled in the doctor's office before going out to Cherokee Canyon to try to pick up the trail of the robbers.

A second outlaw, Jess (Myron Healey), has waited to follow the Range Rider and Dick when they go out to track. He takes some shots at them, then tries to leave them behind as he heads for the ranch where the outlaws are hiding. He might have succeeded had there not been some gunplay between the crooks.

Once the doctor has patched up the gang leader, Cash Corbin (John Doucette), he is not allowed to return to town. He's knocked out and put in the barn.

The wounded Corbin isn't popular with his cohorts, neither for having been wounded nor for refusing to split the money and split up.

Upon reaching the ranch, the Range Rider and Dick force Haley to take them in the house but Corbin has tried to get away with all the money, wounded or not.

The Range Rider leaves Haley with Dick and goes after Corbin, but Jess is waiting behind the barn to waylay Dick.

With Dick tied up in the barn with the doctor, Haley and Jess go after the Range Rider and Corbin.

When Dick and the doctor manage to work their way loose, the doctor heads for town and Dick goes after the Range Rider and the outlaws.

It's chase after chase to wind up this episode.

## "The Chase"
## D: Frank McDonald
## S: Edward Llewellyn
## © 1953

Three bandits steal the mine payroll from Judd (Al Bridge). The Range Rider and Dick hear the shots and give chase. Range Rider goes after two of them and catches Kane (Steve Darrell) but the other gets away.

Dick chases the other and ends up at a ranch. He edges his way in the door and is stunned – and infatuated – when he sees Bonnie Bates (Karen Sharpe), who has just had time to change from her riding clothes before he got there.

When Dick leaves, Bonnie's brother Harper (Paul McGuire) returns and tells her Kane got caught. She is furious. Their father got caught from trusting people.

Back at the sheriff's office, Judd can't positively identify Kane – his eyes aren't what they once were – but the sheriff (Stanley Andrews) says he will hold him for twenty-four hours.

Dick gets back to town and tells them the man he was chasing gave him the slip out by "that cute little gal's ranch."

The Range Rider has the idea of throwing Dick in the cell with Kane to break out with him in order to locate the rest of the gang. So Dick becomes the Panhandle Kid.

He and Kane break out. Kane takes him straight to Bonnie's ranch. Dick has uneasy feelings. Bonnie chews Kane out for bringing the Panhandle Kid, a stranger, to the ranch but she agrees to see him.

When Kane sends Dick in to meet Bonnie, they are both surprised. He thinks he followed her brother the first time and she leads him on. She tells him he doesn't know what she's been through since this morning and, in a way, she's speaking the truth. Kane comes back in and gets his surprise. Dick and Bonnie both turn on him.

Meanwhile Bonnie has sent Harp to get Kane out of jail. He calls through the bars and the Range Rider is waiting. He races out of town with the Range Rider on his tail.

Harp gets to the house far enough ahead to lock Kane in the room with Dick and hide before the Range Rider knocks on the door.

Now they are all at "that cute little gal's ranch" to wrap this story up.

This is one of the episodes that opens with the scene of the Range Rider pouring water on Dick in an attempt to make him a light sleeper. The film is reversed this time because Jocko's gun is on the left side rather than the right.

In a totally irrelevant aside: It was cold when they were filming. Their breath frosts in some scenes.

## "Cherokee Round-Up"
## D: Ross Lederman
## S: Oliver Drake
## © 1952

Chief Black Cloud (Glenn Strange) has been taken captive and caged by some nefarious white men for retrieving horses stolen from the Indians. His warriors are trying to free him when the Range Rider and Dick hear the shooting. They fire into the air to break up the action.

Range Rider tackles one of the braves from his horse and discovers his friend Little Elk (Rodd Redwing), the chief's son. From him he gets an overview of what has happened.

The Indian agent John Stewart (Denver Pyle) and his partner Dorcus McGowan (Gregg Barton) are robbing the Indians. Buckskin (William Fawcett) has written a letter to protest but has not gotten a reply. Little Elk's sister Natcha (Gloria Saunders) works for Buckskin and is also trying to help her brother save their father.

Stewart is also cheating the Army in his horse theft shenanigans.

After a kangaroo court, the crooked agent plans to lynch Chief Black Cloud. When he hears Buckskin's tirade about the letter he is waiting for, he sends white men dressed as Indians to attack the mail carrier and bring him the mail bag.

The Range Rider, Dick and Buckskin work with Natcha and Little Elk to step up to the challenge. They will not only need good tactics but also luck to bring the thieves to justice and save Black Cloud.

## "Convict at Large"
## D: William Berke
## S: M. Coates Webster
## © 1953

Crowder (Harry Lauter) wants Pop Simpson (Stanley Andrews) to sell him the express line. Holdups have become so frequent that the insurance company doesn't want to pay any more claims.

Another wagon has been robbed and one of the masked bandits called the guard, Bill Martin (House Peters, Jr.), by name because they served jail time together. Bill insists he's going straight and the other man calls him a fool. Buck, the driver (Bob Woodward), hears the exchange and tells that Bill is an ex-con when they get to town.

Pop knew about that and defends Martin, as does Carol Simpson (Margaret Field) but Crowder agitates the crowd and the talk gets ugly, so Bill pulls a gun to hold them off and rides away.

Crowder organizes a mob to chase him and lynch him.

The Range Rider and Dick are resting up from the road when Martin rides up into the rocks to hide. The mob rides by but Range Rider and Dick have the drop on Bill, who tells them the whole story.

All three go in to talk to Pop and Carol. They talk Bill into staying around and staying low until the bandits can be caught.

Meanwhile Crowder sends his men in to raid the express depot. He wants that express line and will stop at nothing to get it.

The Range Rider and Dick start for town but run upon the outlaws running from a posse after hitting the express office. They chase them and recover the express bag but the sheriff (Ewing Mitchell) thinks they are the outlaws. He arrests them. Bill decides he must expose himself to danger to rescue the Range Rider and Dick.

Just as Crowder is telling the sheriff he knows the Range Rider and the Range Rider is not the Range Rider, Bill steps out with a gun and frees them. From his last statement, it is obvious to the Range Rider that Crowder is behind all the trouble.

But – he will have to prove that he IS the Range Rider to the sheriff, as well as prove that Crowder is the villain of the piece. His help will come from an unexpected source.

This is one of the few Flying A shows in which House Peters, Jr. gets to be a good guy. He made a wonderful career of playing baddies.

Poor Ewing Mitchell plays another dumb sheriff. He was tapped for a list of them at Flying A before moving on.

### "Dead Man's Shoe"
### D: George Archainbaud
### S: Joe Richardson
### © 1951

The Range Rider and Dick stop a runaway wagon before it goes over a cliff and find Uncle Toby Lee (Tom London) in the wagon bed dying. He tells them he was drygulched. Before he dies, he asks if they will take the real map for his claim to Virginia Lee. It's in his boot.

Range Rider is pulling off his boot when the killers ride up. He and Dick take the boot and make their escape.

The bandits finally give up the chase. Gorham (Denver Pyle) rides up and chews out his henchmen for not getting the map and losing a gold mine worth $2 million. He says whoever took the map will either go to the claims office and file the claim or take the map to the Lee family – if he's honest and dumb.

The baddies split up. Two go to the Lee place to watch for strangers. The others head for the claims office.

The Range Rider and Dick find the map but the landmarks make no sense. Howdy-do Mountain? Chocolate River? They decide to go to the claims office and see if the claims clerk knows these places.

At the claims office, Gorman has knocked out the claims clerk and put one of his henchmen (Francis McDonald) in his place. The gang tries to take the map but Range Rider and Dick get the better hand and revive the real clerk, who tells them the map must be a joke. Howdy-do Mountain and Chocolate River do not exist.

The next step will have to be going to the Lee place to see if Virginia can explain the names. Virginia Lee turns out to be a little girl (Sherry Jackson) who lives with her Aunt Minerva (Louise Lorimer) and her Uncle Toby.

Virginia's Aunt Minerva sends her out and tells Range Rider and Dick that Toby is in his second childhood. No one take his prospecting seriously except him and Virginia. The Range Rider replies that someone took it seriously enough to kill him for the map.

His death is a blow to Minerva, who goes to lie down after the Range Rider says he will watch Virginia. Dick goes to town to notify the sheriff of Toby's death.

The little girl is having a tea party. She tells Range Rider that her doll lives on Howdy-do Mountain and he realizes the names on the map are in a code that Virginia knows.

The two bandits who were sent to watch the place break in, knock out the Range Rider, tie up Aunt Minerva and Virginia and steal the map.

When Dick gets back from town he unties the Lee females and helps the Range Rider get back on his feet and moving. They now know that the map shows the location of a real gold mine.

Dick takes Aunt Minerva and Virginia to the stage to get to the claims office and the Range Rider trails the bandits to get the map. It's not quite that easy but Range Rider and Dick will see it through.

This episode should be titled, "Dead Man's Boot" because the map is hidden in his boot. Toby doesn't wear shoes.

## "Diablo Pass"
## D: Frank McDonald
## S: Polly James
## © 1951

Settlers stocking up at McNair's Emporium may end up afoot at Diablo Pass if McNair likes the looks of their wagons.

Jim Harris (Stanley Andrews) and his daughter Sally (Joan Baxter) have a nice wagon. McNair (Leonard Penn) sends his henchman Bart (Alan Hale, Jr.) to get some men, go after them and get their wagon.

Fortunately the Range Rider and Dick come up in time to run off the bandits, but after they have control of the wagon. Harris was wounded so they take him and his daughter to the closest place, Jess Slattery's ranch, to patch him up.

Slattery (William Fawcett) is not fond of people but he does let them in. Hospitable welcome or not, it's a place to rest while Harris gets on his feet and the Range Rider looks into this situation. Slattery allows that the old-timers are being left alone. It's the settlers in wagons who are being targeted by these bandits.

The next day when the Range Rider and Dick go into town, the Harris wagon has already been repainted and sold.

The Range Rider notices that Bart, who works for McNair, owns the palomino horse ridden by one of the robbers and McNair just sold a wagon to Mr. Robbins. He tips off Robbins, who agrees to work with him before he, too, ends up afoot or dead.

Range Rider manages to talk the unsociable Slattery into working with Harris and Robbins to set up McNair and his henchmen and prove them guilty.

In "Diablo Pass," the daughter Sally is one of those rude, obnoxious children that are supposed to be funny but rarely are. The child is not a bad performer but her role makes this episode an easy one to turn off.

## "Dim Trails"
## D: George Archainbaud
## S: Robert Schaefer and Eric Freiwald
## © 1951

Blake Edmunds (House Peters, Jr.) kills and robs a government agent to get currency plates. He takes the plates to his boss Jed Barker (Harry Lauter), who runs the print shop. Barker has better plans than to mass produce the bills and get caught passing them. He arranges to sell the money to counterfeiter Matt Jessup (Mickey Simpson).

The marshal (William Fawcett) tells the Range Rider and Dick that Jessup is the likely killer. They go out in search of him. They find him dead. It might have been a dead end but Jessup has ink on his sleeve and a broken horseshoe lies close to the body.

Dick goes into town to check out the newspaper office and print shop while the Range Rider goes to talk to the blacksmith. They agree to pretend not to know each other when they reach town, with Dick presenting himself as a law officer and the Range Rider looking to join the outlaws.

The blacksmith tells Range Rider he replaced a shoe for Blake Edmunds, who is in the saloon.

The Range Rider sees a man with ink-stained hands playing cards. When Dick comes in, Range Rider picks a fight with him by making fun of Dick's badge. Dick "introduces" the Range Rider to the poker players by knocking him onto and over the table where they are playing. This beautifully choreographed fight is a highlight of the episode and the series.

When Range Rider throws Dick out the door, the players invite him to sit in. For his first bet he lays the broken horseshoe on the table, which gets Edmunds' attention. Range Rider pretends to have done business with Jessup. He says he's looking to buy money like Jessup did but Barker offers to sell him the plates.

The Range Rider sends Dick into town to steal the counterfeit money from the safe for him to use to buy the plates from Edmunds. Dick gets the money without a problem but forgets to pick up his gloves as he leaves.

The Range Rider needs to make the deal and get out before the outlaws find Dick's gloves or Dick is caught trying to retrieve them.

**"False Trail"**
**D: George Archainbaud**
**S: Kenneth Perkins**
**© 1951**

The Range Rider is taken in by the daughter of an old friend, Sally (Elaine Riley), who is running away with an outlaw, Bert (House Peters, Jr.)

He has stopped for a swim on the way to visit Dick when Sally and Bert stop at the pond to tend Bert's wound. They are being chased by a posse after Bert robbed a stage, but Sally tells the Range Rider they are being chased by Denver Jack's gang.

The Range Rider agrees to ride with Sally, making two horses to be chased, and let Bert slip away, with the understanding that Bert will get the sheriff and meet them at Jeb Thompson's shack.

Thompson (Kenneth MacDonald) flashes a mirror signal for the sheriff when the Range Rider and Sally show up, and soon Sheriff

Tug McGraw's (Edgar Dearing) posse, including Dick, is firing at the shack.

The Range Rider recognizes Dick and calls to him. Dick goes in to parlay. The Range Rider thinks Dick has joined Denver Jack's gang and Dick thinks the Range Rider is the man they were chasing until they talk to each other. Dick goes back to explain to the sheriff, who refuses to believe the Range Rider is an innocent dupe. Sally keeps him a non-believer by going to the window and shooting a posse member.

Sally keeps vowing that Bert is innocent and the Range Rider remains gullible. He agrees to go with her to Bert, but Sally has set him up again and now Bert plans to frame him for the stage robbery – as a *dead* outlaw.

Fortunately when Range Rider and Sally left, Dick went, too, and stayed above the hideout as a lookout. He comes in to break up the action.

Convincing the sheriff that the Range Rider is a good guy will be their last chore to set everything straight.

## "The Fatal Bullet"
## D: George Archainbaud
## S: J. Benton Cheney
## © 1951

Jim Harrison (John Parrish) will hang for a crime he didn't commit if his daughter Leslie (Lois Hall) and friend Panamint (Tom London) don't find the fatal bullet to prove that it is not the same caliber as the one Harrison was convicted of using.

They find it, but Leslie makes the mistake of taking it to her father's lawyer, Steve Carson (James Griffith). The lawyer has reasons for not wanting the truth brought to light and sends two of his henchmen to waylay Leslie before she can get the bullet to the county seat.

The Range Rider and Dick run off the baddies but then Leslie thinks they are chasing her to stop her. She can't keep running because she's been shot. When the heroes catch up, they take her to a cabin to patch her up. Panamint sees them and moves in to save her.

When he starts shooting, the Range Rider puts Dick and Leslie on the road to the county seat while he stays there to stall the assault. Before he can settle Panamint down, the henchmen have heard the commotion and set a trap for Dick and Leslie, then for the Range Rider and Panamint as they try to catch up.

All four are tied up at a cabin. No one will tell where the bullet is, so one of the henchmen rides to get the boss.

The Range Rider works his hands loose and they escape, only to be caught by the boss, Steve Carson.

Time is short. They must escape one more time to save Harrison.

## "Feud at Friendship City"
D: William Berke
S: Buckley Angell
© 1952

Friendship City didn't even have need of a marshal, but it needs one now. There's a range war between the small ranchers and the big Triangle outfit owned by Joel Kirby (John Hamilton), who lives in Chicago. His cousin Seal Kirby (Myron Healey) runs the ranch for him and cheats him steadily, making his cousin believe the small ranchers are the thieves.

The Range Rider and Dick stop on the trail to Friendship City to watch men moving cattle and find a Triangle brand hide stretched and hung to dry where the herders had stopped to butcher fresh meat.

They arrive in Friendship City in the middle of a gunfight between the Triangle men and the small ranchers led by Tom Barrett (William Fawcett) and Lon Gentry (Lee Phelps), who sent for the Range Rider.

In an effort to bring peace they try to approach the Triangle men using a white flag of truce.

Joel Kirby tells them he can't get cattle to market. The Range Rider replies that he and Dick saw a herd of his cattle on the move as they came into town. Kirby doesn't believe him. Range Rider says he can prove it by the hide that was left to season on the trail. He says he can get the hide and bring it back in three hours at the most.

*The Range Rider and Dick West ride into town to help.*

Kirby agrees and sends one of his hands (Tom London) with them. Seal asks again for the location of the hide and sends two men to bury the hide before the Range Rider can get there. Then Seal goes with the hand, Range Rider and Dick.

Seal's henchmen get to the hide and take it down, but the Range Rider and Dick see their tracks and go after them.

When the hand sees evidence that the hide was stretched and hung up just as the Range Rider said, Seal kills him to prevent him from telling Joel and takes his body into town, claiming the Range Rider shot him. Joel grabs a gun and starts to go to war.

The Range Rider and Dick must retrieve the hide and get back to Friendship City with proof of Seal's deceit before the range war turns it into a ghost town.

**"Fight Town"**
**D: George Archainbaud**
**S: Robert Schaefer and Eric Freiwald**
**© 1952**

The Range Rider and Dick ride into what appears as a ghost town because all of the people are at a fight in Benson's barn between Benson's man, Ape Hawkins (Mickey Simpson), and local favorite, Tommy Ryan (Darryl Hickman).

Range Rider smells something phony, especially when the smaller fighter wins handily and Benson (James Griffith) immediately proposes a rematch. Dick comments that the big man looked like he was faking.

Tommy's sister Lynn (Lois Hall) is proud of her brother, thinking he won by skill.

The Range Rider recognizes the fight promoter from the past and knows he's a crook. He plans to send Dick to look for evidence against Benson.

Range Rider and Dick go to try to warn the Ryans but they don't want to believe that Tommy isn't a great fighter. The Range Rider demonstrates, beating him by only ducking and weaving without throwing a punch. Dick doesn't bob and weave as well.

As Dick heads down the road on his search for evidence, he is attacked by two of Benson's henchmen but he shoots Blackie (Mike Ragan) and gets away.

The Range Rider has gone to Benson's office to try to stop the rematch but Ape hits him on the head and leaves him tied up in a mine shaft.

When Dick gets back with enough facts to convict Benson, he discovers the Range Rider missing. He and Lynn follow the tracks to find him while Tommy goes into town for the rematch and bets the ranch on the fight.

Dick and Lynn will have to hurry to save the Range Rider, the ranch and Tommy.

In "Fight Town," the footage of the gag with Dick in a buckboard that flips is used. Dick's guns are on the right side in "Fight Town."

## "The Flying Arrow"
## D: Frank McDonald
## S: Dwight Cummins
## © 1951

The Range Rider and Dick are going to see Grandma Melton (Mary Young). Her grandson Charlie (James Griffith) is wanted for killing a neighbor, Hancock, but Dick knows Charlie is innocent. He hopes the Range Rider can prove it.

Charlie was blamed because Hancock was killed with an arrow and Charlie is known as an archery expert. Now someone is shooting arrows at the Range Rider and Dick. Dick knows it can't be Charlie. He missed.

When they get to Grandma's she tells them Sheriff Clark (Al Bridge) let Charlie go on his own recognizance. Her grandson promised he would be there for the trial. He started back and never got there. The trial is only two days away. A man who doesn't keep his word is worth nothing. Her boy must get back.

The Range Rider finds tracks that show Charlie met someone. He and Dick ride into town to talk with express agent Elwood (William Fawcett), who knows everybody and everything about them. The Range Rider asks about Charlie. Elwood tells him George Turner was probably his closest friend.

On the road to see Turner, the Range Rider and Dick have a run-in with Mel Bard (Douglas Evans) and his cook Spud (Dick Alexander). They are taking the body of George Turner to town. He was killed with an arrow.

Back in town, the sheriff admits to them he will be in a bad spot if Charlie doesn't make it back for the trial. He is the one who released him. And the arrow that killed Turner is like the one that killed Hancock.

Hancock, Turner, Bard and Grandma were having such trouble making ends meet on their ranches that they formed a partnership.

The ranches are mutually willed, making an outstanding motive for murder.

The Range Rider is looking around Bard's place and finds Spud wearing Charlie's boots. He had noted the tracks as unusual earlier at Grandma's. That tells him Charlie is somewhere on the ranch and makes it clear who actually did the killings.

Time is running out. The trial starts in about an hour. The Range Rider and Dick must find Charlie and get him into town – along with the real killers.

## "The Ghost of Poco Loco"
## D: George Archainbaud
## S: Elizabeth Beecher
## © 1951

The Range Rider and Dick hear shots and find a dead man. His money and papers have all been taken. Nearby Dick finds a yellow rose. Tracks show that two riders came in from one direction and then rode out another. A third rider's tracks cross those. They came and went still other ways.

As they are getting ready to take the dead man into town, they see a runaway. The Range Rider goes to the rescue. The young lady is Sally Roberts (Gloria Winters). She is out hunting her father, Professor Hugo Roberts, a specialist in American history who was looking for ruins. When she sees Dick coming with the body she recognizes the horse and cries. Why would anyone kill her father? What if the ghost of Maria Luisa did it?

The third tracks at the scene were the tracks of Maria Hernandez (Donna Martell). She arrives home in a tizzy, saying that the Range Rider is on his way to Solano and she found Señor Roberts shot in the back. Her man Bandy (James Griffith) comments, "That makes four."

Maria sends Bandy and Curt (Dick Curtis) out to scare off the Range Rider, but remember, no killing. She has no clue her men are the killers.

The Range Rider has gone to talk with the sheriff (Bud Osborne), who says the only possible reason for the killings is robbery. The Range Rider doubts that. Then Dick comes in to say

Sally almost has him believing in the ghost of Maria Luisa. The Range Rider laughs but the sheriff tells him it's not laughable.

While they are talking, Curt shoots at the Range Rider and wounds the sheriff. Bandy flees to tell Maria that the Range Rider is headed for Poco Loco while Curt and the Range Rider fight.

After Curt is locked in jail, the Range Rider starts for Poco Loco alone because Dick has to stay and watch the prisoner for the wounded sheriff.

Maria isn't killing but smuggling. She is helping criminals across the border in order to thumb her nose at the people who took her land. But she is in over her head now and the Range Rider needs to help her out.

In "The Ghost of Poco Loco," 1930s cowboy hero Tom Tyler has an uncredited cameo as an Indian in a flashback.

## "Gold Fever"
**D: George Archainbaud**
**S: Elizabeth Beecher**
**© 1952**

Gold! It's a big strike in Calaveras and Tom O'Hara (Stanley Andrews) found a rich vein. Going into Paydirt to file on it, he plans to stop overnight at the Halfway House run by Agnes Drucker (Louise Lorimer) and celebrate.

O'Hara is relaxing with a game of cards when Mrs. Drucker comments on his watch charm, a gold nugget that he found years ago. He can't resist boasting about his rich gold strike, especially when Lon Slade (Harry Lauter) asks him if this one is worth anything.

When Slade hears the reply, he signals a henchman (Mickey Simpson) to get the claim map. Then O'Hara can disappear like the others did.

The Range Rider and Dick come to Paydirt to see Sheriff Campbell (Ewing Mitchell). They are there when Ellen O'Hara (Lois Hall) comes in need of the sheriff's help to find her father. He failed to meet her at the stage.

Before they can begin the search, Slade arrives seeking her. He says her father is a friend who got tied up and asked him to meet

Ellen at the stage. He escorts her away to go to her father's cabin at Cattail Creek.

They only get as far as the Halfway House. The gang needs Ellen to try to force her father to produce the map and turn over the claim. Mrs. Drucker tells Ellen to rest, her father is not here.

After she goes upstairs, Slade tells Agnes about the Range Rider and she sends gunmen to kill him and Dick.

They escape the ambush and finally get to O'Hara's cabin at Cattail Creek. His friend Pat Quinan (Tom London) hurries in and is surprised not to see Tom and his daughter. He tells the Range Rider about the disappearances and jumped claims. Those who disappear have usually played poker at the Halfway House. And, oh yes, that Slade is no friend of Tom's.

Dick pretends to be Hardrock Jones and checks into the Halfway House ready to whoop it up over his new fortune. He and the Range Rider hope their find will be not gold but O'Hara, alive and well.

In "Gold Fever" the same footage of Denver Pyle and Duke York shooting at the Range Rider and Dick, with Jock circling while Dick covers, and then fighting it out is used as in "Big Medicine Man." The footage was probably shot for "Big Medicine Man" because those two are in no other place in "Gold Fever."

## "Gold Hill"
D: William Berke
S: Robert Schaefer and Eric Freiwald
© 1952

Lorette (Gloria Talbot) is worried about the Reverend Norman (John Hamilton). She believes he is in danger and sends for the Range Rider.

The Reverend is making a trip to town to pick up seed and deliver some of the vases Lorette makes to Bannion's store. On the way he is stopped by two of Tillie Jenkins' henchmen (Myron Healey and Bob Woodward) who plan to show him why he needs to sell his land. The Range Rider and Dick arrive in time to fight off the baddies.

Dick takes the buckboard into town to complete the errand. When he unloads the vases, he breaks a couple and Bannion (William Fawcett) refuses them, so Dick takes them home with him.

One of her henchmen points out Dick West to Tillie (Eula Morgan), the lady blacksmith, and she sends him after Dick with another of her men to teach the Range Rider to mind his own business.

They chase him and the buckboard rolls but Dick pony expresses onto one of the team horses and goes back to the settlement.

When the Range Rider and Dick go back for the buckboard, the broken pottery is gone. The Range Rider goes on into town to check on who might want broken pottery while Dick takes the buckboard home.

In Bannion's store the Range Rider tries to buy a vase but Tillie says she has bought them all. He picks one up and "accidentally" breaks it and one of her henchmen jumps him. Tillie cracks the Range Rider over the head from behind to end the store-wrecking fight.

The Range Rider goes back to the settlement and breaks one of Lorette's vases. In the break, gold flecks shimmer. Now they know why Tillie wants the land. Gold!

The blacksmith wants it bad enough to come out into the open and kidnap Lorette. The Range Rider and Dick will have to get her back.

The buckboard spill is the same footage as in "Fight Town." Dick's gun is on the right side.

Additional comedy provided by two Indian boys at the settlement, Matthew (David Coleman) and Mark (Edward Coch) and the Reverend Norman.

## "The Golden Peso"
## D: George Archainbaud
## S: Sue Dwiggins and Vy Russell
## ©1951

Fred Ritchie (Steve Clark) has gone to the Golden Peso Mine, proprietor Dick West, to take a secret ore sample. Bill Mayfield (Jonathan Hale) and his henchman Henry Cooper (Riley Hill) watch him and follow him to make sure he does not get to town with the ore for a second assay. They shoot at him but miss, so they hurry into town to make sure the assay is not made.

The Range Rider comes to the mine and sees that Dick has struck it rich. He goes into town and finds Dick in the Golden Peso Mine Headquarters selling shares in his mine to the towns-people.

Dick introduces Arlene Ritchie (Wanda McKay), who says her father is amazed at the value of the ore samples. It's unbelievable. Undoubtedly the reason he went out for a second look.

Mayfield owns the hotel where Dick is staying and is serving as Dick's banker because he has room in the safe for the money coming in from stock sales. He was also the one who suggested where Dick should look for gold.

The Range Rider is suspicious and goes to Ritchie's office to ask about Dick's find but Cooper shoots the assayer in the back through the window and sets up the Range Rider to take the fall.

Arlene knows something about metallurgy, too, and learns that Dick's mine has been salted. She and the town turn on Dick and the Range Rider.

It will take some doing for them to prove who the real villains are and convince the town.

## "The Grand Fleece"
**D: George Archainbaud**
**S: Sherman Lowe**
© 1951

The Range Rider and Dick see a group of men with masks and cloaks riding up to a shack. Leaving Baker outside as guard, they go in.

Range Rider leaves Dick with the horses and sneaks up for a closer look.

The men are waiting for Petrie (Steve Clark) from whom they are extorting money.

The Range Rider attacks the guard, takes his mask and cloak and pretends to be Baker. When Petrie arrives, he follows him in and, after understanding what is going on, snatches the $2,000 Petrie brought and makes his getaway. The others think Baker has double-crossed them. They learn differently when Range Rider takes Baker to jail.

In town, the Range Rider and Dick return Petrie's money but Petrie is not pleased. Now the gang will want more. As an affirmation of that, while they are talking a rock is thrown through the window demanding more money.

The mayor, who is one of the gang, calls a meeting since the sheriff hasn't been able to catch the extorters. He appoints a committee of his gang members to bring in the crooks.

They plan a "trap," with the committee on guard to close in on the thieves.

When they gather at the snare site the Range Rider suspects that something is wrong. He and Dick start back to town and are ambushed. Then he *knows* something is wrong. They take steps to uncover the gang members and bring them to justice, the mayor included.

## "Greed Rides the Range"
D: George Archainbaud
S: Norman S. Hall
© 1952

Carterville is becoming a ghost town as more and more people leave. Ann Carter (Gail Davis) and her father (Stanley Andrews) will stay no matter what. Ann was born there and she intends to stay.

Rocky Hatch (Lee Van Cleef) and his henchmen harass the Morrows even as they are moving out. Ann comes out to help them, rifle ready.

Just as Hatch aims to shoot Ann in the back, the Range Rider and Dick ride up and Dick shoots the gun from Rocky's hand. When he draws a second gun, the Range Rider takes care of that one and keeps Rocky's guns, shooing the rowdies away. Ann tells the Range Rider and Dick that Carterville was a nice little town until gold was found in the hills.

The Morrows finally get packed up and on the road and Ann is left alone. Her father has boarded himself up inside the mine and won't even let her in when she brings supplies.

The Range Rider and Dick go to return Rocky's guns. The confrontation turns into a slam-bang fight.

When they get back to Carterville, Ann has already left to take supplies to the mine.

Hatch and his henchmen head to the road to the mine to bush-whack her. Rocky is tired of waiting. They attack the wagon but Range Rider and Dick arrive in time to drive them off.

She lets them follow her to the mine but cautions them not to let her father see them.

Ann begs her father to come back home and tells him she's alone now. He seems almost pleased at that news. She's thinks he has greedy gold fever but Hatch is holding him a prisoner in the mine.

Dick goes back with Ann but the Range Rider hides near the mine entrance and hears Rocky giving orders to the man who is guarding Mr. Carter.

At home, Dick goes to put up the buckboard. When Ann goes into the house, Rocky and his men try to kidnap her but the Range Rider appears in the nick of time.

The Range Rider tells Ann that her father is a prisoner, not gold greedy, and they go out to free him and round up the baddies.

## "Gun Point"

This episode seems to have been lost. There is indication it was an early episode. Despite searches of every known source, no dealer has been found that knows anything about it. Not even a cast list is available. Dick did not have a copy of it. Some students of early television history doubt that it was actually filmed.

## "Gunman's Game"
## D: Wallace Fox
## S: Elizabeth Beecher
## © 1951

Two men break prison. An accomplice is waiting with clothes and horses but they are happy to see coffee and grub at the camp-fire where Dick is cooking. Tex Loftis (Al Wyatt, Sr.) says he'll take care of Dick but Dick is a better fighter than Tex anticipated. He calls for help so Joe Matson (Terry Frost) comes up behind Dick and hits him on the head with brass knuckles. Just then the Range Rider appears and chases them off.

The Range Rider asks Dick how he would like a vacation. In

town he picked up a letter from a friend inviting them for a hunting and fishing trip. Dick asks where he lives. When he hears the name Wagon Hound, he chokes on his coffee and drops the cup.

Dick is in trouble. He has been writing to a girl in Wagon Hound, Emily Kyler (Barbara Stanley), and he included a picture of the Range Rider as himself.

Emily has just picked up the picture at the post office and shows it to Sheriff Edwards (Kermit Maynard). He's putting up a wanted poster and cautions her about taking back roads on the way home. The escaped convicts are dangerous.

It didn't matter which road Emily took home. One of the escapees is her uncle, who is now known as Blaze Barnett (Marshall Reed). He has plans to hide out with Emily and her mother until they can get clear of the country.

She protests, but her uncle insists and holds threats to her mother over their heads.

Meanwhile, Dick is stalling to avoid reaching Wagon Hound. The inevitable happens just as Barnett and Matson are robbing the bank. The sheriff is wounded in the gunfire and Dick stays to help him. The Range Rider chases the bandits – right to Emily's ranch.

Emily is delighted to see him and goes out to greet him but her uncle follows. The Range Rider asks about the hot horses. Barnett says two riders went by just a few minutes ago. Range Rider doubts that and he and Barnett fight. Matson ends the fight by hitting the Range Rider over the head just as he did Dick. They take him away from the ranch while he is unconscious. He comes to and goes back to town where the sheriff welcomes him as "Emily's beau."

He is totally confused and has to straighten out the sheriff – and Dick! He says he met Emily and her unpleasant uncle. Then the sheriff is confused, especially when the Range Rider says he didn't meet her mother because she is sick. Emily told the sheriff her mother was fine not three hours earlier.

The three start putting two plus two together and realize they need a plan to save the women from the outlaws. Fortunately, Emily is pretty sharp and able to help them help her.

## "Gunslinger in Paradise"
### D: George Archainbaud
### S: Sherman Lowe
### © 1951

The Range Rider and Dick come upon Noah Geiger (Dick Curtis) and his lawyer Bernis (Denver Pyle) setting fire to a wagon. They run them off.

Investigating the wagon, the Range Rider finds that a hole had been shot in the water barrel. He finds the bodies of a man and a woman who must have died of thirst. He doesn't know it yet but Geiger put the hole in the barrel to murder three people.

Then in the wagon, Dick finds clothes that would fit a young boy. They begin looking to find either the child or the remains. The boy, Donnie (Jerry Hunter), is still alive when they reach him.

Geiger's plan will fail if one inheritor still lives.

The Range Rider and Dick have taken the boy to a nearby cabin and are working to revive him. He's coming around when his scheming uncle and his lawyer come to the door. Geiger wants to take him but Donnie resists and the Range Rider refuses to let him go.

Dick follows the suspicious men, while the Range Rider takes Donnie to Judge Wooley's ranch. Judge Wooley's daughter Sue (Elaine Riley) greets them and takes them to her father (Earle Hodgins) for him to hear the story.

Dick rides in to report that Geiger and Bernis, with the sheriff, are making a search of the ranches hunting the boy. When they reach the Wooley place, Sue puts them off innocently.

The Range Rider and Dick go into Paradise to telegraph for business information and soon learn that Donnie and his dead mother inherited a large sum from a relative in Chicago. The only way Geiger can inherit is if he is the only living heir.

They get back to the ranch too late. Donnie has been kidnapped by his murderous uncle. They must save the boy before his uncle can kill him.

## "Harsh Reckoning"
## D: George Archainbaud
## S: Sue Dwiggins and Vy Russell
## © 1951

A lone rider meets a gang of men and reports to Fulman (James Griffith) that it worked. He says Radford is headed for Evans' place. Fulman and one man go after Evans; the other four after Radford.

The Range Rider and Dick have stopped to climb to the top of a bluff. The Range Rider once thought about being an oil scout and he thinks this land looks like oil country. While they are on the bluff, a man tries to steal their horses. They run him off and chase him to the site of what appears to be a shootout. The gang has set it up to look like Evans and Radford shot each other. Both men are dead.

The Range Rider notices the tracks show at least a half-dozen horses yet two dead men are all they see.

Just as Dick suggests that if the land is rich in oil they fought over it, one of the "dead" men stirs.

Noises come from a nearby shack. Dick goes to check them out while the Range Rider ministers to the wounded man. The man has been blinded from being hit across the eyes by a whip. The noises came not from armed men ready to attack but from Evans' baby.

Radford's foreman Bob Guthrie (Dick Curtis) comes to the Evans place to "discover" the bodies. He is shocked to find Evans alive and the Range Rider and Dick there with him.

When Guthrie gets back to the Radford ranch he tells Radford's daughter Ruth (Donna Martell) that he's made all the arrangements and that Evans killed her father, which she finds hard to believe.

He adds that he met Fulman on the road. He is interested in buying the ranch. Ruth says she can't wait to get rid of it and leave the area. Just so happens Guthrie brought Fulman home with him. Ruth asks him in and the deal is made.

Dick, to whom the Range Rider has assigned the chore of baby care, appears at the Radford place looking for a woman to watch the baby. Ruth agrees to take the infant in for a few days.

The Range Rider has gone to the sheriff (Bud Osborne) with his doubts about the gunfight. Fulman sees them and knows he must move fast.

He drops by the Evans place and makes a deal to take the property off his hands and just happens to have the papers to sign with him. His next stop is Ruth Radford's. Then he will own the whole valley. He knows there is definitely oil on both properties.

The Range Rider is already working to stop his thieving plans and put Evans and Miss Radford back on top.

## "The Hawk"
## D: George Archainbaud
## S: Elizabeth Beecher
## © 1951

The Hawk (Denver Pyle) robs and kills with impunity, thumbing his nose at the law and leaving poems to shame Sheriff Hollister (Tom London). Tired of being played for a fool, the sheriff sends for the Range Rider.

As the Range Rider and Dick are resting on their journey, the Hawk comes up behind Dick and gets the drop on him. When he learns Dick's identity, the outlaw gives Dick a message to pass on. He says he will rob the express office overnight and leave one of his poems especially for the Range Rider. He then escapes.

On the way into town, the Range Rider and Dick hear shots and chase a runaway wagon that the Hawk has just waylaid. The bandit killed Joe Hanford and took the Rafter H payroll. Deputy Clem Rigsby (Gregg Barton) is shaken but able to drive on to town.

When they arrive, the sheriff is meeting with the school board, which is planning a fundraiser. The lawman introduces them to schoolteacher Lettie Parker (Barbara Knudson) and Aunt Sophie Todd (Louise Lorimer), who runs the boarding house where they can stay while in town.

Lettie shows Dick the way to the boarding house and introduces him to Aunt Sophie's brother, Charlie Todd (Denver Pyle), who is an invalid and requires a cane to walk.

The Range Rider, Dick, the sheriff and the deputy plus the express agent keep watch all night but the Hawk/Charlie has no problem sneaking out of his room, robbing the safe and killing the agent.

He leaves a note for the Range Rider telling where he will strike next.

Charlie Todd's masquerade as the Hawk is a good one, especially with his sister to help. The Range Rider has only one more chance to catch him because the outlaw plans to call a halt after taking the money from the school fundraiser.

## "Hidden Gold"
## D: Frank McDonald
## S: Dwight Cummins
## © 1951

The sheriff (Al Bridge) has deputized the Range Rider to bring in a gang that has been robbing and killing for the past three months. Two have been captured but three still remain – one heavy, one tall and thin, and one average. Otherwise, they change their looks.

While the Range Rider and the sheriff are talking, two of them hit Daley's Emporium. They ride off toward Dry Gulch. In a rare incident, the horses are not saddled and waiting so the Range Rider and Dick are too slow to follow them.

Later they go out to track and see that the two met a third rider. As they start to move along, they meet a dude trotting along the path heading for town. He has just passed them when he yells for help. His horse has thrown him.

Dick rides off to catch the horse and the man pulls a gun on the Range Rider. Then he whistles for his boys – the ones who robbed the Emporium, Case "Muley" Harris (James Griffith) and Fall Rivers (Dick Alexander). He introduces himself as Hart Mason (Douglas Evans).

When Dick returns with the horse, no one is in sight. He is reading the ground sign when the sheriff rides up to say all that was stolen from the Emporium was a suit of clothes and a hat. That information, along with what he reads on the ground, tells Dick that the morning robbery was a trap to catch the Range Rider.

In captivity, the Range Rider is being fed royally – or like a condemned man.

Mason wants him to use his tracking skills to locate the Lost Widow mine for them. The owner didn't tell because Fall hit him too hard. They may turn Range Rider loose if they become rich.

Dick and the sheriff have followed the Range Rider's trail to the house where the outlaws are hiding but before they can work their way in, they have been seen and the outlaws hide themselves and the Range Rider in a hidden passage behind the wall.

Farther along the way, the Range Rider is going along with the gang as he works his way to freedom. Dick is tracking them as they move. They need to come together before the outlaws decide they have no more use for the Range Rider.

## "Hideout"
## D: Ross Lederman
## S: Gerald Geraghty
## © 1953

Dick has taken a job with the Southwest Stage Line. The Range Rider comes to town to check on him since he hasn't asked for help solving the problem of the company's missing stages and the stolen gold.

It's a girl, of course. Dick is in love again. Carol (Regina Gleason). Prettier than a prairie sunset. From back East. And she thinks Dick can find a solution all by himself and get a promotion.

The Range Rider solves that problem quickly. He can be Dick's "assistant."

All his "assistant" needs to do is to see Carol and he suspects that Dick is in more trouble than he knows.

The Range Rider goes to the sheriff's office and walks in as the sheriff (Ewing Mitchell) is being told about another missing stagecoach. The lawman has decided Dick must be the tip-off man. Look at all the fancy jewelry he's been buying for that gal.

Dick's been buying it from Jim Crowder (Jim Bannon), who just happens to have driven the last missing stage into the bandits' hideout. Dick's the tip-off man all right – unintentionally. When he gets paid, the stage is carrying gold.

The sheriff comes to arrest Dick, who tries to get away and is stopped by the Range Rider in an impressive action sequence. As the sheriff starts to handcuff Dick, he pushes the sheriff away, runs out the door, jumps the railing, travels a wagon bed in a couple of steps, vaults the Range Rider's horse, lands in his saddle and races down the street. The Range Rider goes right behind him copying every step until he hits his saddle and dashes after Dick. He catches up, grabs Dick by the back of the belt, pulls him from his saddle and holds him suspended as Dick wiggles to get away. No wires, no computer altering in the editing, just exceptional athletic ability. Amazing.

Crowder and Carol meet at the hideout. He thinks it is time for them to pull out of this area but she wants one more haul. He protests that with Dick in jail there will be no more jewelry-purchase tip-offs. She says she will bail him out for one more time. Carol is the hand of iron in the scheme.

They also plan to set up Dick and the Range Rider to take the fall.

Carol tells the Range Rider someone took a shot at her out by the old Sawtooth Mine. He asks why not tell the sheriff, but goes out to check anyway. Dick, out on bail, sees him go and follows.

Once Carol has them in position, she does tell the sheriff, setting them up. He gathers a posse and goes after them. He captures the Range Rider but Dick gets away.

Dick will help the Range Rider escape so they can put a clever plan into action to expose the real criminals.

Ewing Mitchell should be embarrassed, hamming up the sheriff's role like he does in this episode. Or, maybe it's scriptwriter Gerald Geraghty who should blush.

There's a nice cameo here for old-pro Bud Osborne as the stage driver spending found gold pieces.

## "The Holy Terror"
D: William Berke
S: Dwight Cummins
© 1953

"The Holy Terror" is a flashback episode. Dick is wrapping a present for the Range Rider. When the Range Rider tells him they weren't supposed to exchange presents, Dick replies that the Range Rider is always teaching him something. For example, something that saved his life (taking a gun away from someone holding it in your back) during the incident involving Eddie Carlton III (Lonnie Burr), the millionaire's son.

Flashback here to the Range Rider and Dick looking at wanted posters of Sid Naylor (Tom Monroe), Phil Morgan (John Phillips) and Irv Torres (Fred Krone). They hear cries for help and ride to save Eddie Carlton from kidnappers.

Eddie tells them the outlaws hit Horace (William Haade), the camp cook, on the head.

Horace gets to camp to tell Eddie's sister, Lisa (Pamela Blake), that Eddie was kidnapped just as the Range Rider and Dick bring him back.

The Range Rider sends Horace to town to tell Edward Carlton, Jr. (Lyle Talbot) that a kidnapping attempt was made on his son; leaves Dick at the camp with Eddie and Lisa; and goes out to try to pick up the tracks of the outlaws.

Horace rides straight for his henchmen, Naylor, Morgan and Torres, and tells them they need to get the Range Rider before he gets them.

The kidnappers grab Eddie again and hit Dick on the head. Horace himself leaves the ransom note.

The Range Rider does catch Torres, who is trying to shoot him, but before he can tell anything, Horace shoots him "trying to escape."

Eddie is a handful for his captors, reminiscent of "The Ransom of Red Chief."

Mr. Carlton will willingly pay for Eddie's return and the Range Rider planned to deliver the money, but when Horace insists he can do it, the Range Rider is convinced that the camp cook is the outlaw ringleader. It's a matter of getting him to lead them to Eddie and the rest of the gang.

"Indian Sign"
D: George Archainbaud
S: Dwight Cummins
© 1952

The Range Rider has bought a present for Miss Phoebe Sims (Minerva Urecal) at a trading post. Before he and Dick can ride away, a stranger, Jeff Harmon (John Doucette), races up, demands to know what's in the package and tries to snatch it from the Range Rider. They fight and Range Rider leaves him lying out cold on the ground.

As Range Rider and Dick ride to see Miss Phoebe, who keeps house for the sheriff (Edgar Dearing), they meet Bill Lane (Kenneth MacDonald) and his daughter Connie (Elaine Riley), who are traveling peddlers. They are on their way to town to put down money for a ranch.

Lane says they will finish the summer on the road while Connie jumps out to show Dick a new line of merchandise they are selling – Indian goods.

The road to the sheriff's house is filled with interruptions. Harmon is waiting to ambush them farther down the way. They run him off and the Range Rider gives chase but Harmon escapes.

When they finally arrive, Miss Phoebe is delighted with her present. The Range Rider describes the man who attacked them and the sheriff immediately recognizes him as Jeff Harmon, the man he's been chasing for three weeks for an assortment of crimes, including murder.

After hearing the list, Range Rider figures Harmon is looking for something Indian-made.

The Lanes' wagon pelts up to the house. Connie is driving and her father is wounded. The robber ransacked their goods and took the money they had saved to buy the ranch.

Connie takes the Range Rider, Dick and the sheriff to the site of the holdup. When she goes through the scattered goods, an Indian rug with an unusual design is the only item missing.

The Range Rider and Dick trail Harmon. They see the smoke of a campfire where Harmon is talking with a stranger, Steve Bentley (House Peters, Jr.). Steve hired Harmon to get the rug and has built the fire to burn it before the signs on it can be read and prove him guilty of murder.

They catch Harmon, whom Dick takes to jail while the Range Rider goes after Bentley, rounding up the man responsible for this whole crime wave.

In the cast listing for "Indian Sign," John Doucette's name is misspelled as "John Coucette."

## "Indian War Party"
D: Ross Lederman
S: John K. Butler
© 1952

Range Rider is serving as Indian agent for the Wah-Choo-Ka tribe. From the trading post, he and Dick see smoke signals indicating trouble. They ride out to find Chief Young Eagle (Rodd Redwing) and his men planning to kill Frank L. Sieber (Denver Pyle) and Edwin Gurd (Gregg Barton) for mining on reservation land. Range Rider and Dick chase away the Indians.

Sieber tells them he's from the U.S. Department of Survey and is confirming Gurd's right to pit mine copper at Arrowhead Rocks. The Range Rider says Arrowhead Rocks are on the reservation and not open to mining. Sieber replies that's wrong. Arrowhead Rocks are outside the reservation.

Using his tools he shows them that Arrowhead Rocks are just off the reservation.

The Range Rider needs to see Nantana (Glenn Strange), the "wise old owl" of the Wah-Choo-Kas. Young Eagle and his men block the way. Range Rider asks Young Eagle to take him to Nantana for a chance to stop war. Young Eagle replies that he will give him a chance to fight to the death. This is a super fight sequence in which Dick Jones doubles Rodd Redwing to fight with Jocko.

When Range Rider bests Young Eagle, he then demands to see the medicine man.

Range Rider tells Nantana that Arrowhead Rocks are on white man's land and they will pay the Indians to leave them alone while they dig. Nantana says Indians don't want white man's money or gold, just want them away from Arrowhead Rocks.

Range Rider asks why and is told the secret is known only to Wah-Choo-Kas but he can become blood brother to Young Eagle and learn it. Upon learning the secret, he suggests a solution that is unacceptable to the Indians. They attack him and he runs to jump on his horse and escape.

At the trading post, Range Rider finds a letter that hints the surveyor is a phony so he starts to check on him.

While he is gone, Young Eagle's sister, Sparkling Brook (Gloria Saunders) comes to get Dick and shows him that the survey marker has been moved. The would-be land-grabbers see them and try to kill them.

Now the Range Rider must get back in time to save Dick and Sparkling Brook from the baddies, prove the scam the men are trying to run and stop an Indian war.

"Indian War Party" is notable for a couple of scenes.

At the first, Dick has asked Sparkling Brook to the Fourth of July dance. Range Rider says Dick dances like a buffalo in a tea shop. Dick says he's a good dancer [which he was] and she hands him the bolt of material she has just bought to make a dress for the dance. He takes it in his arms and dances with it.

Later Dick doubles Rodd Redwing in an excellently choreographed fight scene with Jocko. Highlights include:

A jump to top of huge fallen log that is about the height of a man.

They clinch, drop, then roll off to the ground.

Dick jumps up and flips himself off Jock's midriff.

He comes back at Jock, who is lying on the ground and catches Dick on his feet and flips him into the air.

Jock boosts Dick up and into a backward roll over the saddle of a horse.

That fight is a stand-out for the entire series of shows.

"Jimmy the Kid"
D: Wallace Fox
S: Milton Raison
© 1953

Dick meets a cute girl, Nell Pearly (Wendy Waldron), by tripping over her and her grandfather's ranch foreman Bill (Denver Pyle) on the way out of the store. He asks to see her again and she tells him there's a barn dance at Allenville the next night. She'll go with him if he will pick her up at the ranch at eight.

Nell and Bill get on the stage to go on to the ranch. Jimmy the Kid (Dick Jones in a double role) holds up the stage and steals the mailbag. Nell thinks it is Dick in other clothes. Bill pulls a gun and Jimmy kills him.

Jimmy took the mailbag, which had no money but did hold a registered letter to Ned Pearly (Steve Clark) with papers proving that he is the owner of his ranch.

Lawyer Parsons (Gregg Barton) comes into the office. When he learns the papers are missing, he tells Pearly he must present those papers before the first of the month or Parson's claim to the ranch will take precedence. Guess who hired Jimmy the Kid to steal the mailbag.

The Range Rider and Dick were going hunting but after Dick saw Nell he forgot to pick up the package with the salt and sugar.

On the road back to town to get it they see signs in the dirt telling of the stage holdup. About that time the posse arrives on the scene. The stagecoach driver sees Dick and points him out to the sheriff (Ewing Mitchell) as the bandit.

The sheriff, who for some reason has never heard of the Range Rider, accuses him of being an accomplice and tries to arrest them both.

They get away and go back to their camp. Range Rider tells Dick to stay in camp while he goes after the real bandit.

Of course, Dick won't stay put. He wants to see that gal.

Jimmy the Kid holds out on Parsons. He wants more money because he killed a man. Parsons says okay, tomorrow. Jimmy goes through the mailbag, finds the registered letter and decides to see if Pearly will pay more than the lawyer to get his letter.

When Dick shows up at the ranch to take Nell to the dance, she screams he's the killer. Her grandfather pulls a gun on him and takes him to the sheriff.

The Range Rider finds Dick in jail and leaves him there while he goes after Jimmy the Kid.

The highlight of this episode is a terrifically choreographed fight between the Range Rider and Jimmy the Kid. (Jock and Dick working together for great effects.)

This is one show that Dick had comments about.

> *We* [Dick and his wife] *were watching The Range Rider episode, "Jimmy the Kid." I played the outlaw in that and Betty got upset. "I don't like you doing that," she said.* [Playing the villain]
>
> *Jock and I did one hell of a fight in it.*
>
> *I died real good in that one – shot in the back running up the wall. I died all over the place.*

It is a good running, dropping to the floor and sprawling out death.

## "Last of the Pony Express"
## D: Frank McDonald
## S: Oliver Drake
## © 1952

Dick West is riding for the Pony Express. At the relay station Mike (Kenne Duncan) asks for news from the East. Dick tells him the Wells Fargo stage has reached Porterville.

As Dick gallops off, Mike calls, "Tell Barstow some of my horses need shoeing."

Dick's run ends at Rimrock. Dick goes in to report to his boss Matt Ryan (William Fawcett) and tells Barstow (Alan Hale, Jr.) about Mike's horses.

Ryan sorts the mail and gives Barstow a letter to take to Tom Benton (Stanley Andrews) at the bank. The letter is from the Department of the Interior.

Matt also has a letter. It's from the main office of the Pony Express, giving him notice that the Post Office may not renew the mail contract with the Pony Express.

Dick doesn't want to give up the Pony Express but Ryan sees the writing on the wall.

It's a tale of the conflict between the Pony Express and the developing stage lines.

The Range Rider comes in from the West driving a stage rather than on a horse. He says Benton is starting a stage line and he's throwing in with him.

Now it's a conflict between the Range Rider and Dick West. Ryan and Benton have an old, old conflict that has kept them on outs with each other for years.

Logan (Leonard Penn) puts in his opinion, saying it's time for an upgrade. He offers horses to the new stage service. But he has his own plans for a stage line that will put both the Pony Express and Benton's stage line out of business.

Benton suggests a partnership between himself and Ryan but Matt won't even hear him out.

Logan has already established a network of saboteurs – the Pony Express employees, Barstow and Mike among the leaders.

The challenge is for the Range Rider and Benton to make Dick and Ryan see that they have a common enemy and must cooperate to survive.

## "Law of the Frontier"
**D: George Archainbaud**
**S: Robert Schaefer & Eric Freiwald**
**© 1952**

The Range Rider and Dick are waiting in the rocks for Judge Henry Moore (Ewing Mitchell) to ride by. The Range Rider wants to protect him from the claim-jumpers and murderers who plague Grubstake by trading places with him.

The judge doesn't know the Range Rider, so when he rides down out of the rocks, Moore kicks his horse into a run.

The judge falls from his horse and hops up challenging the Range Rider to fight by the Marquis of Queensbury rules. The fight is a fun scene with the judge punching and Range Rider dancing all over to stay away from the punches.

Dick, who is still in the vantage point in the rocks, dashes down to tell them someone is coming. The Range Rider quickly gives the judge a knock-out punch.

He and Dick take Judge Moore to a cabin and explain the situation to him. When he first hears of the plan to trade places, he refuses. That would be hiding. When Dick points out that he, the judge, would be playing the Range Rider, the plan has much more appeal.

The Range Rider rides into Grubstake in the judge's clothes and introduces himself as Judge Henry Moore.

Dell Horton (Dub Taylor), Neil Allen (Mickey Simpson) and Otis Levert (Rush Williams) are waiting to greet him. While they are talking, Frank Taylor (George J. Lewis) rushes into the saloon and tells bartender Rod (Boyd "Red" Morgan) to fix a drink for the judge. The usual.

The Range Rider tells them he doesn't drink. They insist, so he asks for a glass of milk. That insults them and the fight begins – with the "judge" using the Marquis of Queensbury rules.

The fight choreography is absolutely delightful. In fact, a certain amount of humor prevails in most of the fights in this episode. For those who recognize the team of regulars in this series, there is also humor in the fact that Mickey Simpson, playing Allen in this entry, drinks the mickey the bartender made for the judge. Mickey got the mickey.

Dick and Moore slip into the hotel the back way, which the judge finds repellant. As they talk about drawing, Dick has an opportunity to show off his gun-twirling skills.

The Range Rider comes in and sets up a target, the judge's hat and coat on a chair by the window. Otis takes a shot at the dummy and the outlaws think the judge is dead until the Range Rider/ Judge Moore comes out – Surprise! He's alive. – and arrests Otis. He turns over Otis and the rifle to be used as evidence to his "secretary," Dick, to take to the sheriff.

Meanwhile, Webb Carver (Stanley Andrews) and his daughter Ann (Lois Hall) have come to town to see the judge. They know him personally.

Before Ann can betray the Range Rider, he embraces her and whispers that he is pretending to be Judge Moore for the judge's protection.

Range Rider takes the Carvers to see Moore but before they can explain their problem to him Claude Portage (Harry Lauter) bursts in and accuses Webb of claiming his mine by forgery. Both men have ownership papers. The Range Rider says he will have to study them and takes them to the judge in the next room.

Dick hurries in to tell them the sheriff has turned the shooter loose and as he opens the door to go to the Range Rider, the judge is overheard saying that the Portage claim is obviously a forgery.

Portage dashes from the room to round up his henchmen. They kidnap the Carvers to take them to their cabin to force Webb to sign over the mine on papers that will be legal.

Still dressed as the judge, the Range Rider goes after them. The judge, who still looks like the Range Rider, and Dick join him to put the gang behind bars.

Dick once complained, "On some of *The Range Riders* they screwed up on the cast. I don't know where they got some of the people that they listed but they weren't even in the thing."

On the author's personal copy of "Law of the Frontier," the cast listing is wrong. It's the same cast as "Let 'Er Buck," but that's not what's printed on the end titles.

Dick often mentioned that problem. No one has ever been able to document for me whether the listings were wrong when originally released or if the error occurred when the series went to public domain.

**"Let 'Er Buck"**
**D: George Archainbaud**
**S: Dwight Cummins**
**© 1952**

The Range Rider and Dick rush to a cabin to meet Marshal Glen Allen (Ewing Mitchell). The marshal wants Range Rider to investigate Webb Butler's Wild West Show. Whenever the rodeo performs in a town, a robbery takes place during or immediately after the show dates.

He shows the two pictures of Butler (Harry Lauter) and his men, Matt Carr (Mickey Simpson), Perry Scott (Rush Williams) and Andy Jones (Dub Taylor).

The Range Rider plans to join the show. Dick wants to be a rodeo star, too, but his partner tells him he wants him to do something else.

After they are out of sight of the cabin, they hear shots and dash back – straight into a fight with a gang of masked men. In the fight, one of the outlaws hits Range Rider with his ring, ripping his face. When he sees that ring again, the Range Rider will know he is looking at one of the baddies.

The attackers ride off and the Range Rider and Dick find the marshal dead in the cabin.

The Range Rider signs on with the rodeo. Butler tells him there is no pay, only prize money. He introduces him to Savage, meanest bucking horse in the show; Vicky Harper (Lois Hall); and Chief Red Sleeves (George J. Lewis).

When Range Rider, Vicky and the Chief have left, the boys jump on Butler for taking on the Range Rider, pointing out that he was one of the men they fought at the cabin. Webb replies it's the best way to keep an eye on him until they can figure out how to get rid of him.

Range Rider has told Dick to watch activities of the rodeo people. Dick reports that every single one of them has made a trip to the bank, including Vicky.

In their hotel room, Dick is sprucing up to look his best at the rodeo when they hear someone in Butler's room next door to theirs. The Range Rider knows Webb is elsewhere. They investigate and find Vicky searching Webb's room. She tells them she wants to see the account books. She is part owner of the show and she thinks Butler is cheating her. As Butler returns, they help her slip out of the room.

The Range Rider and Dick have gone back to the barn where Range Rider is still searching for the ring that cut him when shots ring out from the street. The bank has been robbed and the bank guard killed.

The robbers loop around to slip the horses into the barn when they see the Range Rider running full-tilt that way. Matt stays at the door to block his path. The two fight their way around the room and out into the yard. Webb finally stops them when it looks like the Range Rider will win.

Once again Range Rider and Dick are searching the rodeo headquarters. Now it's for the stolen bank money. When the Range Rider finds it, he takes it to the sheriff and sends Dick out to make Matt think he is taking the loot back to the marshal's cabin, which becomes the site of the showdown with the gang.

In this one, inside the barn where the rodeo crew hangs out, an Iowa banner is prominently displayed on the wall. Iowa was Jock Mahoney's alma mater.

## "Marked Bullets"
D: Wallace Fox
S: Norman S. Hall
© 1951

Dick will turn eighteen tomorrow. He has come to town to see his uncle Homer West (Harry Cheshire), a banker, for an accounting of his inheritance. Bank robbers hit his uncle's bank.

The Range Rider and Dick join the posse hot on their heels. When the sheriff (Ed Cobb) is shot, Dick takes him back to the doctor and the Range Rider continues the chase.

He follows one of the bandits when he reaches a lake and swims to an island with the stolen loot. While the bandit is swimming, the Range Rider marks all the bullets in his gun and belt, then puts them back. Afterward he swims to the island and hides the loot elsewhere after the bandit has left.

The outlaw goes to report to Dick's Uncle Homer. They are conspirators. They planned the robbery together and will report four times the amount of cash stolen to the government to be repaid.

The Range Rider comes back into town and tells Dick he's been following Art Folsom (Don C. Harvey). Dick can't believe it. Folsom is a good friend of his uncle and a big man in town. "And a bank robber," Range Rider adds.

Dick and the Range Rider go to see his uncle about his inheritance. Uncle Homer tells them forty thousand in cash was stolen along with sixty thousand in government bearer bonds, which were Dick's estate. Dick has nothing left.

Dick is furious. His uncle has been reluctant to give him information up until now. He rages, "If you robbed me, I ought to kill you." Bank employee Sharon (Christine McIntyre) hears him say this.

Uncle Homer tells him to come back at eight that night and he and Sharon will go over the account books with him.

Before eight, Folsom comes to the banker accusing him of double crossing and taking all the money. He went back to check on the loot and it was gone. Homer denies all knowledge but Folsom won't believe him. When Homer reaches into a drawer, Art shoots him.

Dick hears the shot as he nears the office, runs in and is knocked out by Folsom, who then changes the spent shell in his gun with one from Dick's gun. Sharon walks in as Dick is getting up and accuses Dick of killing her employer. Folsom comes in right after.

Dick makes a break through the window and when he is gone the Range Rider tells the sheriff about marking Folsom's bullets. When the sheriff asks to see Art's gun, he pulls it on them and escapes.

The Range Rider sets out to catch Folsom and the men in with him on the robbery as well as retrieve Dick's inheritance.

## "Marked for Death"
## D: Ross Lederman (as David R. Lederman)
## S: Dwight Cummins
## © 1951

The Range Rider and Dick ride to meet Vern Underhill (Harry Lauter). His grandfather Cyrus (Stanley Andrews) has sent for them to help.

Vern has been set up for the murder of Piney Baker's foreman. He is running from the law because he fears any trial will not be fair. The Range Rider thinks Vern should turn himself in to Sheriff Rawlins (Al Bridge) rather than stay a fugitive.

Cyrus is furious with the Range Rider for turning Vern in and helps his grandson try to get away but the Range Rider gets the upper hand and Vern ends up in jail.

Baker (Jim Bannon) wants the Underhill ranch. Cyrus has a broken leg and can't manage the range without Vern's help, which is why Baker has set him up for killing the foreman.

The Range Rider and Dick go out to the site of the killing to read the signs. A very distinctive boot heel has made prints in the ground in the rocks, suggesting an ambush rather than an argument between Vern and the foreman.

Baker followed them and knows the Range Rider suspects him so he goes back later to rub out the prints.

When one of Baker's henchmen starts lynching talk, the Range Rider and Dick break Vern out of jail. He goes back to the ranch in time to find Baker there trying to force Cyrus to sell.

The Range Rider and Dick need to hurry to save Vern and his grandfather from the man who won't hesitate to kill to get what he wants.

## "Marshal from Madero"
**D: William Berke**
**S: Joseph F. Poland**
**© 1952**

Two men rob the Gunstock Mine office. The sheriff calls in the Range Rider and Dick West to catch the thieves. They do.

When they take the bandits to jail, the sheriff has gone to the county seat and left his daughter Nan (Margaret Field) in charge. She is also his deputy. Dick is infatuated.

Pete Fowler (Harry Lauter), manager of the local express office, comes in to check on Nan. When he takes a look at the bandits, he winks at them through the bars.

Marshal Collins (Stanley Andrews) from Madero calls to ask Nan to keep a look out for two men who robbed the mail. They fit the description of Reardon (Terry Frost) and Brady (Bob Woodward), who are in the Gunstock jail. The marshal tells Nan he is leaving right away to come pick them up.

The Range Rider tells Nan she will have to turn the men over to the marshal because a federal charge takes precedent over a local. Then he volunteers to take the money to the express office and leaves Dick with Nan.

Reardon tells Nan that he wants to send his watch and ring to his brother in Laramie. They are all he has. He also wants a message sent to his brother saying, "Hope you watch your step better than he watched his."

Since Fowler is in cahoots with the bandits, he takes the watch and ring to gang leader Craiger (Gregg Barton) at the hideout. Craiger is puzzled. Reardon never had a brother. They read the message again and realize he wants them to take apart the watch. They do and find the real message, telling them about the marshal on his way from Madero.

The outlaws waylay the marshal and take his papers. Craiger then takes his place and rides to Gunstock to take custody of the prisoners.

The Range Rider is suspicious of Craiger and trips him up in conversation about the Marshals service. He and Dick set the fake marshal up with their own false words meant for Craiger to over-hear. They follow the fake marshal to the cabin and, with the real marshal's help, trap the bandits.

### "Old Timer's Trail"
### D: William Berke
### S: Paul Gangelin
### © 1953

The Range Rider and Dick run off holdup men. When they talk to the wagon driver, he tells them that the bandits were part of the Diamond Hitch gang.

That gang is the one the Range Rider and Dick are hunting to bring to justice. As they ride they talk and the Range Rider suggests that they search the only area in which the gang has not been active, the Three Trails country. Maybe the unidentified leader is making sure things stay quiet there so that no one will get nosy and look for them in their home territory. They decide to go there next.

An old prospector (Erville Alderson) comes into the Three Trails hotel and asks to sit. He tells the proprietor he wanted to buy this hotel once. The hotel owner, Sims (Charles Stevens), is reading a newspaper. The top headline proclaims a ten thousand dollar re-ward for the missing millionaire with the subhead: "Owen Booth, Mine Owner, Sought by Daughter, Alice Booth." Sims knows im-mediately who is sitting in the room with him.

Sims asks the old man if his name is Booth. "No. Thomas," he replies.

The hotel owner sees a chance for money and tells him if the man really wants the hotel he would sell it to him. Thomas pulls out a wallet loaded with greenbacks.

Just then the sheriff (Stanley Andrews) walks in and asks for his newspaper. Sims has read the paper and wouldn't have the sheriff see the reward notice, so he lies and says the stage driver forgot to pick up the papers.

As the Range Rider and Dick get into the area they see a man riding faster than his horseback skills permit. It's Sims, running to report the location of Booth and get the reward. Another man appears behind him, calling his name and trying to get him to stop. Sims is riding out of control. He hits a tree and dies. The Range Rider and Dick go down to the site where Harrison (Sheb Wooley) also stops and dismounts. Dick picks up a scrap of newspaper with the words "Missing Mill" on it. He puzzles how a mill could be missing.

In town, the sheriff is incensed when Dick suggests that the Diamond Hitch gang could be headquartered in his jurisdiction. He keeps the area bandit free.

The Range Rider and Dick go to the hotel to get a room for their stay and meet Thomas/Booth. After the Range Rider shakes the old man's hand he tells Dick that man has not spent recent time prospecting. His hands are too soft. Then he adds the footnote that this place will be where they start getting nosy. They don't know it yet but they have already met the Diamond Hitch gang leader, Harrison.

Harrison and the gang members are not happy with the hotel transfer. Sims was shipping in ammunition for them in his name. The last shipment should arrive that day so they go to see if they can at least salvage that.

Meanwhile, Booth's daughter Alice (Elaine Riley) has come to the hotel looking for her father. He doesn't recognize her, says she's made a mistake. He's never seen her before.

Rather than staying around the hotel, the Range Rider and Dick are riding out every day looking for signs of the gang. Had they stayed put, the Diamond Hitch would have come to them. Venturing out only gets Dick captured.

When Harrison and henchman Jake (Rush Williams) go to the hotel for the ammunition, Jake recognizes the old man from the picture he saw in a paper. Now they see reward dollars and more coming to them. They don't hesitate. They kidnap Booth and his daughter.

The Range Rider returns and learns what has happened. The sheriff won't help him round up the gang because he's in denial and, with Dick in captivity, the Range Rider has a big job ahead of him.

Watching this episode triggered a memory for Dick.

I noticed Harold Barron doubled me so it was either when I broke my ankle or dislocated my knee. I was hobbling around. I could tell by the way I walked and as soon as I saw him ride I knew it wasn't me. That's the only thing that stood out on "Old Timer's Trail."

## "Outlaw Masquerade"
## D: Wallace Fox
## S: Joe Richardson
## © 1952

Johnny puts on a Halloween mask and jumps out at Dick to scare him. Dick grabs him and turns him over his knee. The Range Rider comes in while Dick is paddling Johnny and stops him. When Johnny whines that a mask is nothing, Range Rider tells him the story of the Halloween gang, vicious killers and robbers who wore Halloween masks.

The episode flashes back.

Three gang members (Denver Pyle, Boyd "Red" Morgan and Robert J. Wilke) make the mail rider's horse shy, throwing the carrier to the ground and knocking him out. They rifle the mailbag looking for one letter, the one from Sheriff John to the Range Rider. One of them reads the letter aloud. The letter contains the message that it is no longer necessary for the Range Rider to come because the sheriff has all the evidence he needs. He is waiting to catch the entire gang, including Belle Clayton (Christine McIntyre).

The henchmen decide to pay Sheriff John (Steve Clark) a visit that night.

John's deputy, Bull Taggart (Gregg Barton) is trying to get his boss to tell him what evidence he has on the gang – after all, he is his deputy – when two masked gang members step in, shoot John in the back and take off.

The deputy becomes the new sheriff. He tells the people he's doing everything he can to find the killers.

It's time for the Range Rider and Dick West to ride in and straighten this mess out.

The gang robs a stage and shoots the driver. The only passenger is a little boy who runs away and hides.

Range Rider and Dick stop the runaway horses and the driver tells them about his sole passenger. They go back to search and find Chuck (Patric Mitchell). He is going to Red Plain from his aunt's in Kansas City to be with his dad, who travels a lot in his job and is staying at the hotel.

Belle Clayton owns the hotel, a hangout for the Halloween gang. The boy's father, Charles Gray (Kermit Maynard), is an insurance investigator. He has gone undercover to dig up evidence and catch the Halloween gang. The people at the hotel know him as Gimpy, the janitor.

Chuck's arrival comes at a most inopportune time. The boy running to Gimpy calling, "dad," immediately after telling Belle that his father works for an insurance company, could make the child an orphan.

The Range Rider and Dick will have to sort this out fast and make a plan to keep Charles Gray alive to reunite with his son. And new Sheriff Bull Taggart has no interest in helping them. Maybe they should find out why.

## "Outlaw Pistols"
## D: Frank McDonald
## S: Arthur Rowe
## © 1952

Kid Laredo (George J. Lewis) has been menacing the Northern Packing Company, robbing its cattle buyers. The episode starts with him killing a guard, wounding the driver and taking the money bag. The Range Rider and Dick hear the shots and rush to the scene. Dick takes off after the runaway while Range Rider goes after Laredo and catches him.

They bring Laredo and the buckboard with the wounded driver and dead guard into town. The sheriff (Stanley Andrews) is impressed with the capture and glad to see the Range Rider and Dick West, who were hired by the cattle company to stop the robberies.

The Range Rider wants to meet Baxter Vale (Sheb Wooley), the company's local representative, so the sheriff takes him to Vale's ranch to introduce him, leaving Dick to guard the prisoner.

In Vale's house, his henchmen Mike (George DeNormand) and Pete (Bob Woodward) are telling the boss that Laredo has been captured. He is more interested in a pair of dueling pistols he has just received. When the Range Rider and the sheriff ride up, Vale sends his boys into the back room.

After the introductions, Vale tells them that the next cattle buyer goes out tomorrow. The sheriff sees the dueling pistols and Vale suggests a shooting competition between the old and the new. Both men hit the target on the nose.

Meanwhile, the sheriff's lovely daughter Mary (Kathleen Case) comes into the office with lunch for the sheriff. Dick is starry-eyed and begins bragging on his prowess in catching bandits. Laredo sees his opportunity to escape and does, leaving Dick and Mary locked in the cell.

When the Range Rider and the sheriff return to find Laredo has escaped, he and Dick go back to Vale's ranch to make plans for the buyer going out the next day. They set a trap for Laredo with Range Rider filling in for the buyer. Vale asks if he's going alone, to which he replies, "How many bandits are there?"

Outside Dick questions his plan of going by himself. The Range Rider tells him, "Richard, you know I'd be lost without you." Dick will be covering his partner's back.

Kid Laredo comes in irritated that Vale has done nothing to aid his escape. They argue over the wisdom of attacking the Range Rider. Laredo insists and Vale agrees, with the condition Mike and Pete go, too.

When they attack, the Range Rider and Dick are ready. They fight and while Dick takes the henchmen to jail, Range Rider goes after Laredo and, ultimately, Vale.

## "Outlaw Territory"
## D: William Berke
## S: Oliver Drake
## © 1953

Most of the people in the territory are supportive of annexation to Texas. Kate Dawson (Minerva Urecal) is leading the group for statehood and working hard to get big rancher King Morgan (Stanley Andrews) to throw his weight in support of annexation.

Kirby Wells (Gregg Barton) doesn't want any changes. Law in the territory would bring his lucrative, illegal operations to an end. His chief henchman is Big Mike (Jim Bannon), who just happens to be Morgan's bodyguard.

Two of Wells' henchmen stop Kate on the road to hold her prisoner until after the election but the Range Rider and Dick, on the way to meet a Lieutenant Stone (Dick Emory), help her get away. Dick goes after the runaway wagon; Range Rider chases the two men.

Kate tells them that the lieutenant is waiting for them at her trading post. When they talk, he tells them that King Morgan is the key to winning annexation. If he supports it people will not be afraid to try to vote. The Range Rider says he and Dick will go out and talk to him.

A henchman (Fred Krone) overhears and tells Wells. The gang gets the drop on Range Rider and Dick and takes them to Kirby Wells. He threatens them and tries to hold Dick hostage but the Range Rider has other ideas. They are delayed but not stopped from seeing King Morgan.

Morgan sees no reason for him to speak out no matter how persuasive the words of Kate and the Range Rider. He is deaf by choice until the Range Rider uses the play of children in the yard of the ranch house as a parable. Then King sees the light and places all his support behind annexation.

That may not be enough to make it happen if Wells and his henchmen get their way.

## "Outlaw's Double"
## D: George Archainbaud
## S: Oliver Drake
## © 1952

Utah Joe (Lee Van Cleef) is on the run. While the Range Rider is taking a swim, Joe steals his clothes and the letter in them that tells Elmer Jensen (Stanley Andrews) and his daughter Lillian (Gail Davis) that the Range Rider will be taking over the job of getting the gold shipments to Santa Fe for Wells Fargo.

Dick is already at the Evergreen Smelting Company telling Lillian that when the Range Rider gets there the bandits will be caught and the Jensens' trouble will be over.

Utah arrives in town, goes into the office and introduces himself to Elmer as the Range Rider. Jensen tells Joe there is half a million dollars in the safe that must be moved. Utah kills Jensen and tries to steal the gold but is run off – with everyone thinking he is the Range Rider.

The Range Rider comes into town in Utah's clothes, grabs Dick and tell him what happened. They plan to meet out of town but Pete (Bob Woodward) sees the Range Rider and thinks he's Utah Joe. The sheriff throws him in jail.

Jim Brandon (Keith Richards) comes in with papers to free Utah Joe. Brandon has been appointed public defender. There's no proof the Range Rider is the outlaw. He could just be wearing similar clothes and be a look-alike.

Brandon is the attorney for Evergreen Mining. He tells the Range Rider to come see him. When he gets to the office, Brandon chews him out for coming into town dressed that way. He tells the Range Rider to buy new clothes and report to Mort Brown (Kenne Duncan) who will hire him to work at the smelter.

Then Utah Joe shows up at Brandon's office. The Range Rider captures him but not before he identified himself to one of the henchmen. Dick takes Utah out of town.

Brandon decides that half a million is worth tipping his hand. Mort pretends to hold Brandon at gunpoint when they go to force Lillian to open the safe but she is too stubborn.

The Range Rider and Dick are now racing against time to save Lillian and the gold and clear up the identity switch.

## "Pack Rat"
## D: George Archainbaud
## S: Samuel Newman
## © 1951

Ben Brown (Francis McDonald) rides up to Joe Harris' ranch ready for trouble. He hears a shot as he approaches the door, goes in and finds Harris dying on the floor. Hearing hoofbeats, he rushes to the window and fires a shot at the vanishing rider. Realizing this doesn't look good for him, he hurries away just in time for Deputy Charlie (Marshall Reed) to see him leaving.

The Range Rider and Dick arrive at Ben Brown's ranch and promptly undertake the rescue of his daughter Nicky Ann (Gloria Winters) from the shed roof by the pig pen. Before it's done both Dick and Nicky Ann are in the pen with the pigs.

They have brought a letter to Ben from his brother, a friend of the Range Rider. The letter is bad news. His brother tells him that he cannot afford to loan him money at this time.

Brown has invited the Range Rider and Dick to eat when the sheriff (Edgar Dearing) and his deputy show up with questions about Ben's activities that morning. Brown starts to run and Charlie shoots him. The wound is not mortal but one severe enough to keep Brown unconscious for a long while.

Circumstances look bad. The sheriff and the newspaper man, Peters (Alan Hale, Jr.), want the story but Ben is still out. The doctor says it will be hours, so the Range Rider and Dick go with Peters to hear the background on the situation.

Peters tells them that Harris had served as an unofficial banker for the community. He had loaned money to almost everyone and had started pulling in the strings so that many were hard-pressed to pay him. A lot of people had reason to want him out of the way.

The Range Rider is puzzled as to why Brown would kill Harris if he was waiting for a letter from his brother that might hold the money to pay off his debt. He and Dick go out to the Harris ranch to investigate. They find a pack rat trading treasures between his nest and places in the house. One of those pieces just might be the evidence needed to prove Brown is an innocent man.

## "Pale Horse"
## D: Wallace Fox
## S: Elizabeth Beecher
## © 1952

The episode begins with the Range Rider narrating the legend of Pale Horse Valley. After an innocent Indian youth was lynched his father put a curse on the valley and all who lived there were dead in six months. Now those who try to enter are found dead at the entrance with the mark of a hangman's noose on their necks. People stay away from the area.

However, the Range Rider and Dick will be going that way. Sheriff Tracy sent for them to help him and the investigation may take them there. As they near the location, an ambusher shoots at them. He misses and Range Rider circles while Dick covers him but the attacker gets away and the Range Rider finds the body of the sheriff who sent for them.

They take his body into town. Hotel owner Blade Sutton (Don C. Harvey) greets them at the hitching rail and says the sheriff lives in his hotel. Sheriff Tracy's daughter Jane (Phyllis Coates) comes out. She is grieved to see her father but calmly sends the body to the undertaker rather than go into hysterics.

Inside the hotel, the Range Rider and Dick fill Jane in on what happened. She asks if the Range Rider knew why her father sent for them. He doesn't know for sure but does have an idea. She knows that her father was working with Mexican police on a two-way smuggling racket, U.S. goods for Mexican silver. He felt he was hot on the trail because there were other attempts on his life.

Marian Knox (Jane Frazee) comes in oozing sympathy but Jane wants nothing to do with her.

Then Jessup (Ed Cobb) comes roaring into the saloon celebrating. He has broken the curse of Pale Horse Valley. He went in and came out alive. But he went in the back way.

Jessup may not be breathing for long. Marion and the man who shot at the Range Rider and Dick exchange glances and he skulks out, only to appear in the window and shoot Jessup.

The Range Rider goes after him. They are fighting when Sutton opens the door, cracks the Range Rider on the head, then slips his henchman inside. When the Range Rider comes to and eases the door open, he is in Sutton's office. He is suspicious.

Sutton sends his henchman for another try at the Range Rider but he misses again when he fires through the window of the sheriff's office where Range Rider, Dick and Jane are going through the sheriff's desk looking for information on the sheriff's search. They do find a map but it is left on the desk and stolen.

Range Rider remembers one of the trails still to be investigated leads to Spider Rock. He and Dick will check it out in the morning.

In the night, a note is pushed under Jane's door telling her to go to Spider Rock alone the next morning to learn who killed her father.

Early morning at Spider Rock it will be "Hail, Hail. The gang's all here."

**"Peace Pipe"**
**D: Thomas Carr**
**S: Virginia M. Cooke**
**© 1952**

Eagle Bend needs a doctor so the Range Rider suggests that Joe Gillette (Paul Fierro), son of the Navajo chief, set up practice with his medical degree in town.

Joe and his family don't even make it to town before the harassment starts. Blackie (Robert J. Wilke) and Spider (Boyd "Red" Morgan) try to spook their horses on the way.

The Range Rider and Dick help them move in with many of the townspeople walking by to jeer. The Range Rider is a little slow here when he doesn't see that this is going to be an uphill drive.

Dr. Joe and his wife (Gloria Saunders) and son (Louis Lettieri) deal with all varieties of prejudicial acts, which are egged on by Mark Tyler (Henry Rowland) and his henchmen. He is planning a land swindle. Playing the race card will help put him exactly in the position he wants to be and Dr. Joe's move set him up.

The Range Rider will need to find a way to trump his ace.

## "Red Jack"
## D: Wallace Fox
## S: Joe Richardson
## © 1951

Five men have been killed with no explanation. Jack Doyle (Don C. Harvey) has served a jail term. He and his wife Ruby (Christine McIntyre) moved for a new start but have never been welcomed and now a killer is leaving red jack playing cards by each body.

The townsmen suspect Jack because of his name and his red hair.

The sheriff (Ed Cobb) and two leading citizens, Mark Lord (Steve Clark) and Asa Gordon (Stanley Blystone), come to the Doyle house to ask for Jack's alibi. Ruby's statement isn't good enough.

The Doyles swear Jack was at the ranch but Lord still wants them out of town. Gordon admits there is no true evidence against Jack and tells him he will help him if a mob is after him.

Lord is the next man killed. The Range Rider and Dick hear the shots and find the body on the road. They are puzzled by the jack of diamonds lying by the body but go after the red-headed man they see galloping away.

They follow the horse's track to the Doyle barn. Jack is inside checking out a noise he heard there. He demands to know what the Range Rider and Dick are doing there. Jack and the Range Rider fight and Jack's right wrist is injured. Range Rider thinks Jack is the man they followed and is going to take him to jail but Ruby gets the drop on him and Doyle gets away.

He rides straight for the Gordon ranch for help. Once Gordon knows Jack came there without telling anyone, he traps him in the cellar and tells his henchman that Red Jack is still is business.

The Range Rider and Dick have taken Ruby to the sheriff's office. When Range Rider hears about the series of killings, he begins to doubt that Doyle is Red Jack. When Red Jack attacks the sheriff's office, he knows Doyle is not the man. That man has complete use of his right hand.

Gordon sends Red Jack after the Range Rider and Dick when they go back out to investigate the site of the ambush, but they are smarter than the killer. Once they catch him, the Range Rider knows who is behind Red Jack and where to find him.

"Red Jack" has two snippets of Flying A stock footage: The scene with the Range Rider pouring water on Dick and the scene in which Jocko circles while Dick covers and runs out of bullets.

By watching carefully, it is also possible to see Dick fighting to keep his chase horse running on the trail. Must be one of the dove hunting horses he mentioned.

## "Renegade Ranch"
**D: Wallace Fox**
**S: Robert Schaefer and Eric Freiwald**
**© 1952**

The Range Rider and Dick hear a shot and ride to find a man dead in the road, ambushed in the back from the rocks. The Range Rider sees distinctive tracks in the hiding place that indicate a cane.

Uncle Cameron Carpenter (Ewing Mitchell) comes home and asks why his niece Ann (Wendy Waldron) has baked a cake. She reminds him that her brother Tim will be home from school today. With his education, she wonders if he will be able to get the water out of the flooded mine.

The Range Rider and Dick have taken Tim Carpenter's body into town. The sheriff (Steve Clark) can't imagine who would shoot Tim. He doesn't have enemies. He must, because Dick points out that he was shot in the heart from ambush and the Range Rider adds that the bullets were soft-nosed to shatter on impact.

The Range Rider and Dick go out to break the news to the family. Ann dissolves into sobs. The uncle thanks them, then heads into town to see Morgan Harris (Gregg Barton), who runs the saloon and is also fronting for him to buy the Carpenter ranch.

Cameron has Harris call in Pete (Robert J. Wilke) and Blackie (Boyd "Red" Morgan) to kill the Range Rider. He hands them soft-nosed bullets he has brought.

He also insists that Harris go back to the ranch to offer Ann one more deal, which she refuses. At that point Harris wants out but Cameron follows him back to town and catches him with the Range Rider, who was waiting for Harris.

With both of them tied up in the back room of the saloon, Dick has to hurry to get the Range Rider and save Ann, who is now on her Uncle Cameron's murder list.

This episode starts exactly the same as "Right of Way." The footage, including dialog and tracks showing a cane are used.

## "Right of Way"
## D: George Archainbaud
## S: Robert Schaefer and Eric Freiwald
## © 1951

The Range Rider and Dick hear a shot and ride to find a man dead in the road – ambushed in the back from the rocks. The Range Rider sees distinctive tracks in the place in the rocks where the killer hid. It looks like the mark of a cane.

Crutch Bellows (Dick Curtis) comes into the saloon for a drink and beats up Jess (Wes Hudman), one of the hands on the Harper ranch, with his crutch.

The Range Rider and Dick bring in the dead man and ask for identification. Pete Harper (Kenne Duncan) sees the body and claims it as one of his best hands, the third one killed from his outfit.

Harper has trouble getting hands. Crutch makes a job there unhealthy. Pete asks the Range Rider and Dick if they are interested in working and they say they'll pass. Then the Range Rider sees the tracks Crutch leaves in the dirt. That changes his mind and he says he'll let Harper know if he wants to work after all.

Crutch sends two henchmen (Robert J. Wilke and Denver Pyle) out to keep the Range Rider and Dick from working for Harper. They are not easily discouraged and show up at the Harper ranch to work, only to be welcomed with gunfire from the owner, Beth Harper (Margaret Field). Pete is her uncle.

When Pete arrives and Beth hears about another killing, she vows she will sell the ranch to Bellows and stop the deaths.

Pete says Crutch owns the land on both sides of the ranch but wants the strip that belongs to the Harpers.

Crutch chews out his henchmen for getting beaten. He wants that land because the railroad is coming in and needs it for the right of way. They tell him the Range Rider is a man to deal with. He went crazy when one of them "hit the kid." Crutch decides to use Dick to stop the Range Rider from helping the Harpers.

When Range Rider and Pete go to look over the ranch, Beth sends Dick and Jess on an errand, then goes to see Crutch to sell the ranch.

Bellows' henchmen attack the wagon, kill Jess and kidnap Dick. They show up at the house with Dick as a captive just as Beth is about to sign over the ranch.

Now the Range Rider and Pete have two reason to raid Crutch's place. They must be careful to avoid the trap he has set for them.

"Right of Way" was one of the early episodes. Footage from that episode is used in several later ones. The opening scene was used again in "Renegade Ranch." Same man killed from ambush. Same tracks with cane or crutch.

When Crutch sends his henchmen to stop Range Rider and Dick from working for Pete Harper, the exact same footage is used to stop them from working for the Pete Harper in "Secret of the Red Raven."

When the henchmen try to waylay the Range Rider, he drops out of a tree onto both of them. That footage was used several times.

The buckboard spill with Dick is the same as in "Gold Hill" and "Fight Town."

The final fight is done with cudgels (a crutch and the handle of a pitchfork), an interesting variation.

## "Romeo Goes West"
## D: George Archainbaud
## S: Dwight Cummins
## © 1952

The Range Rider and Dick are hold up watching the ghost town where Gold Rush Johnny (Francis McDonald) lives. They think Ben Colton (George J. Lewis) and his henchmen (Myron Healey, Gregg Barton and Dick Alexander) are down there and fear they may have harmed Johnny.

They have. He's been slapped around until he is unconscious. The bandits want his riches, but now they must wait until he regains consciousness to make him reveal the hiding place.

The Range Rider has just told Dick he plans to sneak into the town in the night when a wagon pulls up at the shack they are using. It is "Pettigew's World Famous Shakespearean Co.," complete with Henry Irving Pettigew himself (Earle Hodgins) and his grandchildren, Juliet (Eilene Janssen) and Orlando (Mickey Little).

The Range Rider quotes from *Romeo and Juliet* and makes a hit with Juliet. He quotes an offer of money to rent Pettigew's wagon and makes a hit with him.

The Range Rider and Dick dress up as traveling players and drive the wagon into town. One of the henchmen (Healey) sees them coming and calls the others. They enter with flamboyance – doffed hats, flowery language, sweeping gestures. One look around is enough for the Range Rider, who sees the gang and figures they'll stay put long enough to come back with the law, but Colton wants a show. They are performers; here is an audience.

The Range Rider and Dick acquiesce and go back to the wagon, really to make a getaway, but the kids are stowaways who jump out and run inside. Now they're trapped – with an audience insisting on Shakespeare.

Colton wants to hear *Romeo and Juliet* so they opt for the balcony scene with the Range Rider as Romeo and Dick as Juliet.

Orlando sees the gang knocking on the walls for money and finds Gold Rush Johnny still alive. Then he points out a misanchored piece of scenery. They pull it from the wall and coins pour to the floor. They tell the outlaws it is stage money.

The job for the Range Rider and Dick keeps on growing. Catch the Colton gang. Save Gold Rush Johnny. Protect the kids. Perform Shakespeare. Find a way out. And all of this with Dick in a Juliet costume and the Range Rider in Romeo tights! It is one of the most entertaining episodes.

## "Rustler's Range"
## D: Wallace Fox
## S: Elizabeth Beecher
## © 1951

The Range Rider and Dick hear shots and find a little girl, Rusty Lyman (Sandra Valles), who is alive, and her escort Charlie, who is not, lying in the road. Rusty can't tell them what happened. She was suddenly jerked from her horse, then blankness. She does know that her pony, Lightning, is missing.

After the Range Rider takes Rusty home, he goes back out to check the road for sign and meets Thelma Frost (Ruth Brady), an

*This copy of the sketch used in this episode hung on the wall of the Jones' den.*

artist who has recently come to the area, and her brother Vincent (Denver Pyle). Rusty had been posing for her before she was attacked but Thelma doesn't mention that.

When the Range Rider leaves, Thelma chews Vincent out for killing Charlie and reminds him that she is the boss. Then they hear shots. The Range Rider is after their henchmen. He captures Pate (Duke York) and takes him to jail.

Rusty's father, Jim Lyman (Ewing Mitchell), tells the Range Rider and Dick that horse thieves have been plaguing the area. The sheriff (Al Bridge) tells him there have been three murders as well as thefts at the Slash D, Running J and Rafter O. All were killed by blows on the head.

Range Rider sees Thelma Frost ride in and asks the sheriff about the Frosts. He believes they are nice people. Dick always likes to meet the ladies, so the Range Rider takes him to the studio to meet Thelma. While she is sketching Dick, the Range Rider notices paintings from the three ranches where killings took place. He also notices items from Argentina in her studio.

Vincent and his henchman come to break Pate out of jail. When the Range Rider runs out after them Vincent knocks him out with a bolas, weapon of the Gauchos.

That ties it together for the Range Rider. He knows the Frosts are running the horse theft gang and asks for Jim Lyman's help to set a trap.

**"Saga of Silver Town"**
**D: Ross Lederman**
**S: Orville H. Hampton**
**© 1952**

The Range Rider and Dick hear shots and race to break up a holdup. The Range Rider wings one of the bandits but the other two get away. He sends Dick to trail them with directions to meet at the fork in Lone Canyon later.

Range Rider stays to check on the victims and drive the wagon. Placer Dan Meighan (Clayton Moore) and Miguel Ruiz (Edward Coleman) have been robbed of the profits from silver jewelry made and marketed by the people of La Plata.

In La Plata, Sheriff McCandles (Lane Chandler) comes to the wagon to see what happened. He and Meighan talk about whether or not to just quit. The Range Rider asks them to give it one more try with his and Dick's help. They agree.

When Range Rider and Dick meet, Dick shows his partner the Spanish Sword Inn and tells him that he trailed the bandits there. They talked to the girl who runs the place before riding out on fresh horses.

The Spanish Sword is supposed to be haunted. Soapy (William Fawcett), the bartender and cook, won't even sleep in the building. He sleeps in a shack out back. "With a bottle?" asks the Range Rider.

In a fun display of the athleticism of the stars of this series, the Range Rider and Dick scare the inebriated Soapy away. "Señor Soapy, I am after you," they chime.

Soapy's exit clears the way for Dick to take over as chief cook and bartender. He knows nothing about how to do either.

The Range Rider comes into the inn for breakfast. When a customer grabs Dick to shove a plate of bad-tasting food in his face, the Range Rider steps in to help. Dick points him out to Sue McCandles (Nan Leslie), the sheriff's daughter who runs the place, as Rusty Rivers, "fastest gunslick in the West." (Dick's alias is Wildcat Wilson.)

Dick's bartending skills are worse than his cooking. Scenes involving them are played with broad humor. When Chuck (Fred Krone) asks for a drink with a kick, Dick throws liquid from many bottles into a glass and calls it a "Tombstone Tornado." Chuck spits it out for "not enough kick." Dick tries again and comes up with a "Santa Fe Swizzler." Chuck takes a drink and does a beautiful spinning down flat floor fall as the drink knocks him out.

While Dick is struggling to bartend, Andy (Harry Lauter), the sheriff's deputy, comes in to speak to the boss. He points out Rusty Rivers and chastises her for letting a gunslinger hang around but that's camouflage to get them to the office to talk. They are the bandits and are planning another holdup already.

Range Rider goes into town to talk to Meighan. After watching Sue at the inn he is suspicious of all the sheriff's connections. Meighan tells him the townspeople have decided to send out another jewelry shipment the next day. The sheriff is riding guard. Range Rider has an idea for a trap.

Early the next morning Andy brings the outlaw the Range Rider took to jail to the inn. The deputy has learned Rusty Rivers is still locked up. The bandit identifies the Range Rider as the man who captured him and the fight is on. With so many against one, the Range Rider is knocked out, tied up and left behind with Dick and another henchman while the others go to steal the jewelry.

Dick will manage to free the Range Rider but he must do it quickly to be in time to set and spring the trap to send the sheriff, his daughter and her cohorts to jail.

Dick remembered the bartending scene with a smile.

*I was making "Santa Fe Swizzlers" at the bar and Fred Krone was my taster and he did a wonderful knock-out fall. He just wilted. That was a Pat Buttram-type scene.*

*We'd do anything we could think of that hadn't been done.*

There's a lot of humor in this one: Soapy, Dick's cooking and bartending, then as the final confrontation is set up, Dick has dumped water on the Range Rider while he is tied to a chair. When the Range Rider hurries Dick to untie him, Dick says, "You promise you're not gonna hit me." Range Rider never does promise.

Dick worked with a bad ankle in this episode. He pointed out to the author during a viewing that he had on athletic shoes rather than boots when he flips over the bar.

## "Sealed Justice"
## D: Wallace Fox
## S: Robert Schaefer and Eric Freiwald
## © 1951

A man opens the door and shoots Sheriff Winters. The sheriff's dying words are, "Get the Range Rider." Of course, he means get the Range Rider to help as he has already sent for him. When the deputy, who becomes Sheriff Barton (Kermit Maynard), hears the words he thinks the Range Rider shot the sheriff.

The Range Rider and Dick arrive but because the letter indicated trouble they enter town separately. Dick goes into the sheriff's office, asks for Sheriff Winters and says he sent for the Range Rider.

Burton thinks Dick is the Range Rider and tries to arrest him. Dick leaves town with a posse on his tail. Dick meets the Range Rider on the road and gives him a brief rundown. The Range Rider sends him to stay with Gator Joe (Chief Yowlachie) up in the hills to hide out until the Range Rider can see the sheriff's daughter and make a plan.

When the Range Rider gets to Joyce Winters' (Barbara Stanley) house he tells her he came to help get the man who killed her father. She thinks he did. Her rancher friend Chad Walker (Marshall Reed) pulls a gun on the Range Rider, who then shows Joyce a letter from her father asking for his help in capturing Ringo Massey. Then she realizes her mistake.

Before he leaves, he tells her he'll be at Gator Joe's if they learn anything.

Chad can't beat it back to his men fast enough to send them to Gator Joe's after the Range Rider to get the letter. He is Ringo Massey.

Because Gator Joe won't let Dick out of the house to help fight, the Range Rider is beaten up and the letter stolen right in front of Gator Joe's house.

It's a mishmash of mistakes and false identities before Ringo Massey is unveiled and Sheriff Burton realizes who is on the side of right and who has pulled the wool over his eyes.

## "The Secret of Superstition Peak"
**D: William Berke**
**S: Elizabeth Beecher**
**© 1952**

Joe Baldwin (Steve Clark), on his death bed, is telling his friend, Ed Curruthers (Lyle Talbot), of a crime of his past when he and three others killed curriers and stole the treasure of the Emperor Maximillian years before. They buried it on Superstition Peak, drew a map and each man kept a piece. Two were killed and he has their pieces of the map.

Baldwin gives Curruthers the maps, assuring him that the curse will not be on him because he is innocent of wrongdoing. But he warns him to look out for the cougar tracks, the whistling stones and the blue flame.

Curruthers accepts the maps and he and his daughter Hope (Pamela Blake) go to Silver Bull, the town near Superstition Peak.

When the Range Rider and Dick ride into town, Hope is berating Sheriff Dennis O'Halburn (Francis McDonald) for not searching for her father. He and a local man, Harry Cooper (Lane Chandler) went to the mountain the day before. Cooper came back through town at top speed, not even stopping to speak, and her father hasn't been seen since, though his horse wandered into town.

The sheriff, who is on crutches, invites the Range Rider and Dick into the office so he can brief them on why the town is so deserted.

Lena Peterson (Cecil Elliott), sends her Indian henchman, Nouri (House Peters, Jr. in an uncredited role), to blow a poison dart through the window and get the Range Rider. The Range Rider goes after him but is stopped by Gus (Tom Monroe), setting up a fight opportunity.

The sheriff notes that the Indian and the man the Range Rider fought both work for Lena Peterson. The viewers have already seen her take Curruthers prisoner.

Hope gives the Range Rider and Dick permission to search her father's room for the map. They find it but don't tell her before going to check out Superstition Peak. She sees them leaving and follows.

Now she *and* her father are in harm's way as the Range Rider and Dick search the mountain and play tag with the villains in order to save both father and daughter; solve the mystery of the flames, stones and cougar tracks; and bring Peterson and her henchmen to justice.

## "Secret of the Red Raven"
**D: Wallace Fox**
**S: Oliver Drake**
**© 1952**

The Range Rider and Dick see a holdup taking place and chase the robber, Joe Larkin (Gregg Barton), to a cabin. Once inside, he rips off his mask and cape and begins firing at them.

Jim Harper (Kermit Maynard) comes in from the back and tells Joe that he'll have to get out. Old friendship only goes so far when a man turns bad and Jim wants him gone before his daughter Susan (Sherry Jackson) gets home.

Joe shoots Jim in the back and runs out the back way.

When the Range Rider and Dick rush the cabin, they find Jim dead on the floor with a bullet in his back and believe he is the outlaw they were chasing. They think they killed him when he started to run.

Just then Susan comes in and begins to cry. The Range Rider hides what he believes to be the truth, that her father is a bandit, and tells her that her dad was a brave man.

Susan tells him that she and her father were getting ready to leave to go help her grandfather, who is in trouble.

The Range Rider and Dick take Susan to her grandfather, Pete Harper (Steve Clark), who is seeking the lost vein of gold in the Red Raven mine. They find him in the general store telling storekeeper Hilton (Ewing Mitchell) that someone is trying to stop his searching.

Susan rushes to her grandfather and Range Rider and Dick tell him that her father has been killed.

Pete and his granddaughter leave for the ranch after inviting the Range Rider and Dick to stay with them. They linger to buy Susan a present.

When all have left the store, the storekeeper goes to the back room where he tells Carl (Denver Pyle) that Jim Harper is dead and the Range Rider and Dick plan to help Pete out. Hilton sends Carl and another henchman (Robert J. Wilke) to discourage the pair from working for Pete Harper.

When the henchmen fail to scare off the Range Rider and Dick, Hilton says they will have to use stronger methods. Carl suggests killing Pete but Hilton says that won't work at all. If the sheriff starts investigating around the mine, he may discover the passageway under the border that the storekeeper has been using for smuggling.

Hilton then gets a break. Joe Larkin comes into the store. Hilton asks him how he'd like to make $500. As far as Susan and her grandfather know, Larkin is still a friend. Susan calls him Uncle Joe.

Hilton needs Larkin to help him get the ranch. Susan trusts him and her grandfather would do anything to protect her. Susan would go with her Uncle Joe freely.

Joe goes to the ranch and tells the little girl and her grandfather that the Range Rider and Dick killed her father. They can't deny it because they believe he was the outlaw they were chasing and shot.

Pete runs them off the ranch. They go to Jim Harper's cabin. Pete takes his son's gun and goes there, too. The Range Rider tells Pete what happened and their concern to protect Susan from knowing her dad was a robber. Harper believes him. Now they are suspicious of Joe. How did he know Jim was shot in the back? The sheriff had kept that secret.

They go back to the Harper ranch to find Susan gone. Under the pretense of taking her for a ride, Larkin has kidnapped her.

The Range Rider and Dick go separate ways to search for her and Pete stays at the ranch. Sure enough, Carl comes to get Harper to take him to Susan. He tells the grandfather he needs to bring the deed to the ranch.

Meanwhile, Dick has found the outlaws' hideout but has been captured. Now it's up to the Range Rider to stop Hilton's scheme.

In "Secret of Red Raven," the scene in which Denver Pyle and Robert J. Wilke try to stop the Range Rider and Dick from working for Pete Harper was likely shot for "Right of Way." It is the only close-up of Wilke in the episode and it is the same footage.

The great fight gag with Range Rider bodily throwing one of the henchmen into the other to knock them down and out is also in "Right of Way."

## "Shotgun Stage"
**D: George Archainbaud**
**S: Joe Richardson**
**© 1951**

Outlaws led by McNally (Harry Lauter) stop the stage, kill the driver (Boyd Stockman), and kidnap the passenger (Rand Brooks), after making sure he has papers that prove his identity, Donald Austin. They take his papers and his clothes. One of the bandits (House Peters, Jr.) puts on his clothes, takes his papers and gets back into the stage before the gang spooks the team into a runaway.

When the Range Rider and Dick stop the stage, the fake Austin introduces himself and tells them he inherited the Shotgun stage line. He pretends to be shocked at the wildness of the area. They take him into Shotgun.

In town, Kathy Roberts (Elaine Riley) and her grandfather Duckbill (William Fawcett) come to meet the stage and are surprised to find the Range Rider driving. He tells them there was a holdup and the driver is dead.

Duckbill tells the Range Rider and Dick that McNally is behind all of their problems. He has a competitive stage line and wants to take over.

When the fake Austin hears the situation, he is more than ready to sell out to McNally, as he is getting paid for the impersonation to do just that.

Kathy protests that if McNally had a monopoly it would finish off the town. Austin doesn't care but the Range Rider points out that a man who prides himself on being a business man wouldn't take the first offer, and he volunteers himself and Dick as stage drivers until the line gets on its feet. McNally may be thwarted for the moment, but is still up to his crooked tricks.

He plots to stop Dick and the Range Rider from driving the stage and, when they are not ready, Kathy decides to drive the stage herself rather than lose the permit.

McNally sends men after her but once they extricate themselves the Range Rider and Dick aren't far behind.

McNally still has a hole card that the Range Rider must trump before an action-packed stagecoach race and the triumph of the good guys.

In "Shotgun Stage" there is a bit of unintentional humor when Harry Lauter tells House Peters, Jr. he picked him for the job because he is the same size as Rand Brooks. When the two men stand side by side it is obvious the same clothes would not fit them both.

## "The Silver Blade"
**D: George Archainbaud**
**S: Dwight Cummins**
© 1952

The sheriff (Earle Hodges) has sent for the Range Rider and Dick to capture the Silver Blade. The outlaw's trademark is a silver dagger in his belt. Every other aspect changes.

While scanning information on the Silver Blade, the Range Rider notes that he and ex-cavalry captain, Cass Faraday, have the same general description and the same expensive tastes.

Then an invitation for the Range Rider is thrown through the door of the sheriff's office. Don Manuel Valero (George J. Lewis) asks for his help. He says that he was shot in the leg by the Silver Blade and warned away from his ranch. As he had not been there since childhood, he doesn't understand. But he also knows that no one there would know him. The Range Rider will take the place of Don Manuel.

The Range Rider arrives at the ranch complete with much luggage, a haughty and domineering attitude and a manservant named Ricardo (Dick West).

The Silver Blade's henchmen have made themselves at home in the big house. They hear the caravan coming and Cullen, the foreman (Myron Healey), sends Barker (Dick Alexander) and Daley (Gregg Barton) to the bunkhouse before the owner can enter.

Later in the bunkhouse, the gang is unhappy about being turned out of the house. They plot to get rid of Don Manuel and make it look like an accident.

They are not very good at that.

Ricardo enters to announce that Don Carlos Mendoza (Francis McDonald) and Señorita Maria Mendoza (Charlita) are in the parlor.

One of the things the Range Rider did not know was that Don Manuel and the girl next door, Maria, were betrothed at a very young age. In the ensuing years Maria has found a new love and wishes to be released from the promise. The Range Rider has no right to release her as he is not Don Manuel, but now his job includes capturing the Silver Blade *plus* figuring a way to free Maria before he is forced to fight a duel for her hand.

Dick had a great time playing Ricardo. He intentionally tangled in the hat and overdid the accent. He remembered the episode fondly.

*The one [Range Rider episode] that I liked, that I had the most fun with was when Jocko was playing the Spanish don and I was his manservant. I had on a serape and a huge sombrero and I kept getting tangled up in the serape and the chinstrap. I'd fight that thing and Jocko would just keep going on, never look at me and I'd just have ball upstaging him.*

*I was in the background fooling around with that big hat. I got caught up in the curtains coming through the door. They just turned me loose on that one. I worked that hat in the draperies until it was just about worn out. The first time it happened it was an accident and I said, that's a good one, so I did it over and over again.*

*Though he wasn't a participant, Dick liked the swordplay at the end.*

*A man named Faulkner was a fencing master who ran a school in Hollywood. Doubled just about everybody in their fencing scenes and we got him and he did a good one.*

*I did some fencing for a while until those lunges got to me. I fell on my face and I said, "That's enough."*

## "Ten Thousand Reward"
## D: Ross Lederman
## S: Curtis Kenyon
## © 1951

The Apache Kid's gang separates and a few draw away the guards, leaving the wagon carrying the gold vulnerable.

When they hear the attack, the guards start back but the Range Rider and Dick are closer and run off the gang, wounding the Apache Kid (Steve Conte) in the gunfire exchange, and stop the runaway wagon.

At the Apache Kid's hideout, he and his gang are discussing the riders who thwarted the robbery. One says it was the Range Rider. They decide it's getting too tough with all the lawmen and bounty hunters. The Kid has a ten-thousand dollar reward on his head. It's time to quit. But, the Kid says, after one last job.

The Apache Kid has an idea. One of his men will turn him in for the reward. After they get the money, they will break him out of jail.

In the marshal's office, the Range Rider and Dick are making plans to go after the outlaw when Deputy Al (Harry Lauter) comes in with rancher Harper – really gang member Cliff (Jim Bannon) – who has captured the Apache Kid.

Marshal Thomas (Al Bridge) is happy. He tells Harper/Cliff he's getting a big reward. The Range Rider is suspicious. He asks for details of the capture. The fraud tells him that he's a stranger who got lost and saw the cabin. He looked in and saw the Apache Kid, whom he immediately recognized, alone and got the drop on him. To avoid the gang, he brought him through Devil's Pass.

When Harper/Cliff and the sheriff go to the bank to arrange for payment of the reward, the Range Rider starts listing the things in the story that don't fit. He and Dick go out to the area the bandit described to investigate.

They sneak up on the cabin. It's empty. Dick goes in and sits at the table. The Range Rider can't see him clearly. There's no trace that anyone looked around the window. The story seems fishier and fishier. When they go to Devil's Pass, there are no tracks of passage, but there are plenty on the road. Not just the prints of the broken shoe on Cliff's horse and one more, but a group of men rode with them.

They go back to tell the marshal.

After talking it over, the plan is to play along. If Harper/Cliff is honest there'll be no harm done. If he's one of the gang he may lead them to the rest. The gang will learn the Range Rider cannot just shoot, but is also pretty smart.

This one screams for a critical note. On the Marshal's Office sign the word is misspelled "Marshall's Office." The marshal's name is not Marshall.

**"Trail of the Lawless"**
**D: Wallace Fox**
**S: Oliver Drake**
**© 1952**

The Range Rider and Dick wake Sheriff Dan (Ed Cobb) in the middle of the night so people won't know they are in town.

Range Rider shows the sheriff a newspaper with a lead story about outlaw Curt Manning (Jock Mahoney in a double role) being released from prison. The sheriff remarks that Curt and the

Range Rider look enough alike to be twins and Range Rider responds that they are. Manning is his twin brother who ran away from home. The sheriff has a big file on the case.

The Range Rider took this case in hopes of straightening out his brother.

Manning is known to be a member of the Red Dawson (Don C. Harvey) gang that headquarters at Maw Manning's outpost in the town of Gunsight. The sheriff said he knew Maw Manning (Sarah Padden) and always thought she was a nice lady. He figured Dawson moved in on her and she couldn't get the gang out. Dick suggests that maybe the Range Rider can help Maw Manning as well as his brother.

The plan is for the Range Rider to take his brother's place. The sheriff helps them by stopping the stage and telling the driver (Bob Woodward) he wants to talk to his passenger. They go up into the rocks where the Range Rider takes his brother's clothes and leaves him confined with a guard while he goes to Gunsight. When the sheriff returns the passenger, it's the other twin.

The Range Rider goes to Maw Manning's and gets a warm welcome. (Dick has planned to meet him there pretending to be the Yuma Kid, a friend from prison.) The gang's warm welcome is mainly because Curt is the only one who knows where the $100,000 from the robbery that put him in jail is hidden. Bullet (Duke York) and Hank (Boyd "Red" Morgan) don't like the way he has changed. For that matter, neither do Red and Maw. They all want the money and the Range Rider has no clue how to find it.

In fact, he clueless about a lot of things in Curt's life, including Doris Burton (Phyllis Coates). The telegram telling him she will be on the stage the next day is not good news.

He sends Dick to meet the stage with the message he had to leave town. Dick tries to warn her off Curt, saying prison had changed him, but she defends him like a tiger. It is only when she discovers that he lied about being out of town that she gives him back his necklace, his ring and the letter she had been holding for him.

At last! The whereabouts of the money! The envelope holds a map. If the money is there he and Dick will have bait for the outlaws.

The Range Rider will have to own up to a lot of deceptions and clear up misconceptions to resolve all of the confusion in this case. And resolution may be delayed when his twin brother escapes his guard and returns "home."

## "Treasure of Santa Dolores"
## D: William Berke
## S: Orville H. Hampton
## © 1953

Saber Jack Tyrell (Sheb Wooley) coerces El Pescadito (Charles Stevens) to break out of prison with him. The Little Fish once rode with El Latigo and Saber Jack wants the map to El Latigo's treasure that he believes the old bandit has. El Pescadito resists. The treasure belongs to the Mission of Santa Dolores. Saber Jack slaps him around, gets the map and finally shoots him.

The Range Rider and Dick find him in time to hear his dying words.

They are all on a crash course when they head for the mission.

Saber Jack planted an accomplice, Hans (Rush Williams), at the mission while he was in jail. Hans has searched and found nothing. Saber Jack thinks the map will reveal the mission's secret.

When the Range Rider and Dick come to the mission, Padre Sebastian (Erville Alderson) tells them the story of El Latigo in a flashback that shows the famous bandit (Lee Van Cleef) raiding, and the circumstances that led him to give his treasure, the fortune Saber Jack is now seeking, to the mission.

The Range Rider and Dick stay at the mission, hunting the treasure for the padre but finding trouble from Saber Jack and his henchmen. However, right will overcome and the Range Rider finally solves the mystery of El Latigo's treasure.

After watching "Treasure of Santa Dolores," Dick commented, "That's one with my good friend Fred Krone in it. He was just getting started."

## "Two Fisted Justice"
## D: Frank McDonald
## S: Ewing M. Brown
## © 1953

Mark Sanders' (Sheb Wooley) railroad henchmen are evicting Matt Johnson (Stanley Andrews) and his granddaughter Betty (Kathleen Case) from their ranch. They have a court order to take the place. When Johnson resists, they begin beating him with a whip.

Steve Brady (George J. Lewis) and two other ranchers arrive in the nick of time and stop them. They tie Sanders' men to a tree and are whipping them when the Range Rider and Dick appear on the scene.

The three ranchers run. The Range Rider cuts down the railroad men, then he and Dick chase the ranchers. They catch Steve and his pards, who refuse to talk, so they go back to get the story from the men being whipped. When they get back to the spot, the men are gone. There's nothing to do but give back the guns and continue to town to meet Judge Blake (Sam Flint), which was their original objective.

Meanwhile, in town, Sanders is meeting with his henchmen and Sneed (Francis McDonald), the county surveyor, who is part of the scheme. Sanders has upped the reward on Brady to $2,500. He figures one of the ranchers will double-cross him for that.

In the hotel, Judge Blake tells the Range Rider and Dick he wants to settle the problems between the railroad and the ranchers. Feeling that the railroad has not dealt fairly with them, the ranchers are harassing the railroad workers and delaying progress.

Blake wants the Range Rider and Dick to find the ranchers' hideout and bring Steve Brady to federal court so that he can testify to the irregularities. When Dick sees the picture of Brady, he groans, and the Range Rider tells the judge they had the man and let him go. Blake sends them back out to find the ranchers and get Brady to the state capital.

Tracks from the Johnsons' wagon lead Range Rider and Dick to the hideout, where the Range Rider attempts to sneak Steve out before the others can stop them. Brady fights him and Matt gets the drop on Dick and the Range Rider.

The Range Rider tries to convince Steve they are working for Judge Blake, not Mark Sanders. He tells him about the increase in the price on his head. Brady is doubtful but agrees to go with them in the morning.

Pete (George DeNormand) leaves, saying he wants to tell the other ranchers what's going on but he's really headed for Mark Sanders and the $2,500 reward.

On the road to the state capital, the railroad men stop them and insist, at gunpoint, on going into town to the marshal (Kermit Maynard). The marshal agrees that Brady is the Range Rider's prisoner but will wait till the morning before releasing him.

The Range Rider and Dick go to send a wire to the judge. As they are leaving the telegraph office, they see Sneed skulking into his office furtively. They follow and discover him burning records. He confesses everything, including a plot to kill Steve Brady in a jailbreak.

The Range Rider and Dick have to hustle to save Steve and uncover Sanders as the villain.

## "West of Cheyenne"
**D: William Berke**
**S: Oliver Drake**
© 1953

The Range Rider and Dick are stopped by two men who tell them to get out of the territory. They fight. One of the baddies falls over the cliff. They chase the other to the blacksmith shop at Slade's Crossing. On the way, the horse splashed through mud, making it readily identifiable. The horse is standing by the shop but Slade (Tom Monroe) denies knowing the owner.

The Range Rider and Dick report to Jean Snyder (Pamela Blake) who introduces them to Tim Riley (William Haade) and Larry Rand (House Peters, Jr.), part of her crew contracted to string telegraph wire to Slade's Crossing. The telegraph company has sent the Range Rider and Dick out to check on the situation. For the past two weeks progress has been delayed by sabotage.

Jean sends Tim back to the blacksmith shop with the Range Rider and Dick to take a look at the horse but the horse has been cleaned up and is gone by the time Slade and the Range Rider finish fighting.

Larry and Jean ride up. Larry tells Jean he is going to the mill at Deer Creek to check on more poles and will meet them at camp. The Range Rider and Dick go out to escort the supply wagon in.

Larry goes not to the mill but to Steve Gray's ranch to report in. Gray (Lyle Talbot) is the man who bid against Jean for the contract. She believes, and rightly so, that he is the one behind the sabotage.

He sends Slade and Hal (John Phillips) out to destroy the wagonload of wire coming to camp but the Range Rider and Dick arrive in time to save it.

However, someone blows up part of the wire and pole supply that night in camp. Jean telegraphs asking for a time extension to complete the work.

The Range Rider sees Larry rolling wire off a cliff. Now he thinks Tim's suspicions are correct. Then he catches the telegraph operator in a lie. He will have to come up with a clever plan to combat the forces trying to stop Jean's work.

## "Western Edition"
**D: Frank McDonald**
**S: Orville H. Hampton**
© 1953

The Range Rider and Dick are rushing to get to Woodville. Their friends, Harris Townley (Lyle Talbot) and Dora Wickersham (Elizabeth Harrower), are getting married. They run *The Argus*, the town newspaper. Townley has asked them to help track down a gang of rustlers while they are there.

They ride in just as the ceremony is ending and the couple is leaving the hall. People begin firing guns in the air in celebration and suddenly Townley falls dead in the wagon. The shot was not from the celebratory pistols but from a rifle on the roof of a building.

Dora is now the owner of *The Argus*. Three of the town leaders, Judge Barrett (Sam Flint), Turner Shelton (George Meader) and Monroe Bradford (Tom Monroe) meet with her in the office. They doubt her ability to keep the paper publishing but she assures them she is going to try. The Range Rider and Dick will stay on and help her.

Townley was killed because of his investigation into the missing cattle. He told Dora as they were leaving the ceremony that he had all the evidence he needed to identify the rustlers and blow the town wide open. The Range Rider has the notes from Townley's pocket but neither he nor Dora can figure them out.

The Range Rider asks about the three men in the office. Each could have had more wealth or power had *The Argus* not exposed them publicly at some point. Dora mentions that Bradford and Harris had an argument right before Harris went to Junction City to check some records.

Dick struggles with the type in the back shop. After a couple of tray spills, the Range Rider sends him out to be a reporter.

When Dick sees Susan Campbell (Anna Lee Carroll), who runs the lunchroom, he starts building himself up as a great newspaperman, Scoop West. He tells her he knows who killed Townley and why. He has the notes right in his pocket.

Two of the rustlers (Fred Krone and Bob Woodward) hear him and believe him. They kidnap him and take him to Hurley (Marshall Reed), the actual killer, to beat the information out of him.

The Range Rider has gone to Junction City to visit with Tom Parsons (Francis McDonald), the cattle buyer, who tells him Bradford ships regularly using three brands. He also says that any number of people would like Harris Townley out of the way.

Back in Woodville, the banker thinks the Range Rider is joking when he comments on the number of cattle Bradford ships.

Then Susan comes into the newspaper office to return Scoop's badge, which he left at the diner. She tells the Range Rider that Scoop rode off with two men. He asks which way did they go, then goes after him.

With the Range Rider's intervention, he and Dick get the best of the three rustlers and take them to jail.

The Range Rider knows that Hurley is the killer but wants the man behind him. He decides to use the power of the press to reveal the man behind the murder.

## "Western Fugitive"
## D: George Archainbaud
## S: Oliver Drake
## © 1951

The Range Rider and Dick are on their way to Gunsmoke to help June Rogers (Margaret Field) when they see Sundown Saunders (Robert J. Wilke) staggering afoot down the road. When they stop to help him he takes their horses but Rawhide throws him and breaks his neck.

Range Rider finds a letter from lawyer John Barton (Kenne Duncan) on him, introducing him to Sam Dawson (Dick Curtis), the man June is having trouble with, as a man good with a gun who will do any job for enough money.

Neither Dawson nor Jane knows Sundown, so the Range Rider takes the letter and rides into town masquerading as Sundown Saunders.

He comes into the saloon as June, her brother and other ranchers are confronting Dawson about blocking the trail to prevent their herds from getting to water.

Dick comes in shortly after the Range Rider, identifies him as Saunders and accuses him of killing his partner, the Range Rider. They fight and Dick leaves with the ranchers when they go.

The Range Rider stays to hire on with Dawson as Sundown.

Barton comes to Gunsmoke with the falsified land transfer for Sam so that the crook can run out the other ranchers and gain control of the entire valley.

The Range Rider must be a master juggler to pretend to follow Dawson's orders while protecting Dick and the ranchers and keep Barton from identifying him as the Range Rider in order to stop the valley from bursting into range war.

Dick found amusement in watching "Western Fugitive."

*Maggie was in it – Mrs. O'Mahoney, Jocko's wife. She was supposed to be shooting a gun and was real serious when she was in the gunfight. I slowed it down to watch because I couldn't believe my eyes. She would fire the gun straight up in the air, down at the ground, over to the right then to the left, never shooting where the person was supposed to be that she was shooting at. Never where she was looking. I thought that was funny.*

# *Buffalo Bill, Jr.*

After *The Range Rider*, Dick was still under contract to Gene Autry. He didn't know how the idea for *Buffalo Bill, Jr.* came about, but he speculated:

> *Gene would get together people for brainstorming sessions and I imagine it was in those brainstorming sessions that they came up with the name, came up with the judge, came up with the little girl to attract the feminine side of the audience. Then they wanted somebody handy so they wouldn't have to stop the camera to get a double to make it look like he knew how to ride. Since they wanted somebody handy and I was still under contract, they said that's what Dick can do. The brainstorming sessions are the reason they did what they did* [with the *Buffalo Bill, Jr.* show].

Dick was very handy but his co-stars were an older man, Harry Cheshire, and a little girl, Nancy Gilbert. With no stunt-capable co-star, Dick's action work had to be performed with company stuntmen or guests. Fortunately there were many of those on hand and there was plenty of opportunity for Dick to display his impressive athletic talent. As a result, there was only a little less action in the *Buffalo Bill, Jr.* shows than had been in *The Range Rider*.

Retrospectively, Dick thought the *Buffalo Bill, Jr.* shows were better thought out. A number of fans don't see it that way, loving the rough and tumble action of two stars working together regularly.

*I think the stories are better on the* Buffalo Bill, Jrs. *and the acting is better. I think the whole thing is better than* The Range Rider. The Range Rider *was too new and too hurriedly put together. That's got to hurt.*

The premise for the show involved Judge Ben "Fair and Square" Wiley, for whom the town of Wileyville was named, and his adopted children, Buffalo Bill, Jr. and Calamity. He had found the Bridger [their actual surname] kids wandering in the Black Hills after their parents were killed in an Indian attack, the boy carrying his baby sister wrapped in a buffalo robe. Hence the name, Buffalo Bill, Jr.

It never mentions why the judge chose the name Calamity [maybe after Calamity Jane], but it certainly fit her. Again and again she precipitated a calamity, although in some episodes she was able to help out.

Dick speculated how Nancy Gilbert got the part.

*I asked Nancy, "How'd you get tied up with Gene Autry?"*

*She said, "I did one of his movies at Columbia."*

*I guess out of all the kids that were there, he got along better with her than with anybody else and he decided that she would be good for the show.*

Wileyville was a nebulous, constantly moving town. In "Fight for Geronimo," the Judge says he found Bill wandering in the Black Hills carrying Calamity. In "Redskin Gap" Wileyville is a few miles north of the Mexican border. In "Six-Gun Symphony" it's not that far from Flagstaff. In "The Fight for Texas" it's obviously in Texas. In "Secret of the Silverado" it's back on the Mexican border. The Apaches appear in several episodes, placing the town in Arizona, and in "Grave of the Monsters," Wileyville is by the Navajo reservation. The town moves for the convenience of the story. It really gets around.

Each episode began with an introductory narrative by Judge Wiley, setting the stage for the story. Several of those involve real life outlaws of the Old West.

Whichever historical outlaw shows his face in whatever episode is always described by the Judge in his beginning-of-show narrative as "the worst" of the Old West outlaws. In "Trail of the Killer," he's Billy the Kid. In "Redskin Gap," he's Butch Cassidy. In "Kid Curry – Killer," he's Kid Curry.

Though Bill was only a kid, he could track, was an expert shot and horseman, and generally handier than many a man who appeared in the show. Interestingly, Bill's horse is never tied when he needs to ride in a hurry.

One of the running set of lines in the series was when Bill tried to stop Calamity from tagging along or sent her home was for him to say, ". . . for two very good reasons. First, you're a little girl, and second . . . ." It varied here. Maybe, "you're my sister," or "it's dangerous," or "you're bound to get in trouble," or he had saved the "little" and the line was, "you're just a kid." But there were always two reasons, which made absolutely no difference because she did exactly what she wanted to do not what she was told.

Another reoccurring incident was Calamity in a wagon with a runaway team that Bill had to chase and stop. One of those was used behind the front titles.

Dick said:

> *The opening of Buffalo Bill, Jr. was a runaway wagon with Calamity in it. That was one shot that was used over and over again. That's when I did that transfer from my horse to the ironing board between the two horses and grabbed the reins and hollered "whoa." They called it an ironing board [because] they mounted a six-by-one board that was clamped onto the tongue of the wagon so you'd have a wider space to stand on rather than the three or four inch tongue.*

Various actions would set the sequence up and off, but it ended the same way, with Bill stopping the wagon and chastising Calamity for not being careful.

Still another running gag was for the judge to turn everything the kids did wrong into a court case. Time and time again he sentenced them to jail, then suspended the sentence. Or they were sentenced to wash dishes, cook meals, clean the store, and other household chores for a week or a month. Though the judge was an

*Bill rescues Calamity, one more time.*

upright man, many times when the general store became a court-room, the term "kangaroo court" might be applied.

The general store was everything. The sign on the front read:

*Wileyville*
*General Store*
*Groceries* ¤ *Hardware* ¤ *Dry Goods*
*Judge Ben (Fair 'n' Square) Wiley Prop.*

Under that a smaller sign announced:

*Justice of the Peace*
*Town Marshal*
*Physician & Surgeon*
*Blacksmith*
*Haircuts & Legal Advice*
*By*
*Appointment Only*

The family lived behind the store and much of the interior action took place in the store itself or in the living quarters behind.

Dick discussed "fights that tore up the store."

*Afterward we probably moved to another set while the prop people rebuilt that set. We choreograph what we're going to do and we walk through it so the cameraman knows what we're going to be doing and when they say "action" it goes. We go through the whole routine without stopping unless something drastically goes haywire and then we'd have to start all over again. Once you get up speed, you don't slow down for nothing.*

*The only thing I don't like about fighting in the general store is that we go into shelves where all the canned goods are and you'd hear empty cans. None of those cans had anything in them and they sounded empty and it used to bug the heck out of me.*

There were some spectacular fights in the series. Dick talked about onscreen fights.

*Gotta keep our stuntmen working. I know every time I look at a* Range Rider *or* Buffalo Bill, Jr. *and it's an indoor thing, first thing I do is scan the scene and see what kind of furniture's in there. If there's a stove in there I know there's going to be a fight and the stove's going to get demolished.*

*Sometimes you'd hit something that hurt. People who are afraid of getting hurt or are not acrobatic you can always tell. When they take a punch they look backwards to see where they're going to go. If I see that, if I'm working with them, I'll stop and cut it right there. In the real world you don't look back to see where you're going.*

*Fight scenes in older films were just swinging their arms around beating on nothing.*

*Today people say, "I did all my own stunts." They don't know what a stunt is. They sit down in a chair without looking at it. That's a stunt. Nobody knows how to go backwards without looking where they're going. It drives me up a wall, somebody takes a punch and they look back where they're going to fall. You get clocked in the face and you get knocked down, you don't have time to turn around and look back where you're going to go. You just go where you're going.*

Dick enjoyed doing the action and talking about it, even years later. He got together with friends in the field and rehashed the work.

*Jack Williams was a nice guy and he was one hell of a horse-faller. His horse falls were so terrific that he made the cover of Life magazine with one of them.*

*Fred [Krone] and I and Jack were analyzing and talking about how you do something and what should have been done. If I could do it over this would've made it look better. I like doing that.*

*I'm real critical about that stuff. I say, "Damn, I wish I could do that again. Get it right." The camera angle is the whole secret to it.*

*I got one that I wanted to do and make sure that the camera angle was just right. The camera angle was just right; it was just too far away to see it. I wanted to do the whole thing without any cuts when I overtook the stagecoach and transferred to the stagecoach. Then up over the top, down into the boot pull the horses up and yell "Whoa" right into the camera. But the transfer, I did a hell of a long leap, more than just riding up and grabbing hold of the coach; I had to dive for it. It was cross screen the way it should be done but it was too far away. You couldn't tell what was going on.*

*That was like when I wanted to do the bulldog, transfer, horse fall – Bang! Bang! One, two, three – three different gags in one shot. It started from too far away and when the gag was done we ended up where we wanted to be, right in front of the camera and you could see it was us, not some cockamamie double, but it was too far away. That's the trouble with the little screen. Big screen sells better.*

This gag stayed on Dick's mind because he brought it up again later in conversation.

*There's something that I wish I could've done over again. I did a transfer to a runaway stagecoach. It was so far away that I couldn't see the transfer. I'm chasing the stagecoach and all of a sudden I'm pulling up the team. I had to back it up and it was way in the background in the distance.*

*I did a transfer, bulldog and I did it into the camera. It was all washed out.*

*I guess I'm too critical because I watch them [Buffalo Bill, Jr.] now and think, "Damn. I wish I could do that one over. It either was shot from the wrong camera angle and the gag was lost or it just didn't work out the way I thought it would. I'm too critical when I watch them.*

Dick was far-and-away too critical. Watching his work validates the fact that it is amazing. In addition to the fights and the horsemanship there was the combination, fights that took place in a wagon or on a stagecoach. Those were common in the *Buffalo Bill, Jr.* episodes. Dick had some comments.

*I didn't fall off the coach. I was the hero. The bad guy fell out the back end.*

*Fights on top of stagecoach or wagon were controlled very carefully. Once you got on the insert road with the camera car doing about 35 MPH you had to have it choreographed right to the step. Fighting on top of the coach, that's ok because you've got a flat surface to work on. It doesn't get the bumps and rolls because the insert road is very smooth.*

*Coach only one that gives you problems. Flatbed wagon you've got sides. You don't have that on top of a coach, just a handrail. Ones we did on top of the things either went down into the boot and then came up and fought on top and maybe went to the back and down into the luggage rack.*

*Dick transfers from saddle to stagecoach with a long leap.*

*Dick jumps from rocks onto a wagon.*

*Dick bulldogs a stuntman.*

*Buffalo Bill, Jr. publicity still of Dick on Chief. This is probably the horse that would stand still for dialog.*

For a man who didn't remember a time when he couldn't ride a horse, Dick cared very little for them. They weren't pets, they were tools of his work, or with good ones, partners.

He talked about the horses used on *Buffalo Bill, Jr.*

*I only used three black horses in* Buffalo Bill, Jr. *I had a trick riding horse. I had a good-looking horse that would stand still for dialog and I had a chase horse.*

*Calamity only used one horse – that white pony. Ponies are usually spoiled rotten, got a mind of their own, they don't want to do what you want them to do. That's what I don't like about ponies.*

*Front cover of Buffalo Bill, Jr. #2.*

*Back cover of
Buffalo Bill,
Jr. #1. Note
the well-read
condition.*

Toward the end Nancy did a lot of her own riding but at the beginning they had a little girl who doubled her most of the time. She
was the daughter of one of the two real good stuntgirls. There were
two girls that were every bit as good as the Eppers [noted family
of stuntmen and –women] were and it was one of their daughters
who doubled Calamity on Buffalo Bill, Jr.

Harry Cheshire couldn't get up on that mule. He used a ladder. I don't
think he could've possibly put a foot in the stirrup and pulled himself up.
He had an old ladder that was put together with tree limbs.

Dick commented that, "Some *Buffalo Bill, Jr.* episodes were put
into comic books."

According to Boyd Magers in his column "Comic Book Cowboys" in *Western Clippings*, the *Buffalo Bill, Jr.* comics began in

*Buffalo Bill, Jr. advertising Milky Way candy offer.*

March of 1955. Each issue contained two stories and had a cover photograph of Buffalo Bill, Jr. The series ran for thirteen issues. Eighteen of the twenty-six stories were adaptations of television episodes, the first issue kicking off with "Fight for Geronimo."

Many of those comics are still available through comic book dealers.

*Buffalo Bill, Jr.* only ran a season and a half, forty-two episodes. Dick explains the reason and continues with a tale of his regret.

*When it came time to renew* Buffalo Bill, Jr., *Mars Candy was the sponsor. Their stipulation was that they have the same time slot, same day, same station and CBS says OK, we'll give you that but we want twenty-five percent and Gene says, there isn't twenty-five percent to dicker with so good bye, off into the sunset we went.*

*I found out too late that he sold all his interest in* The Range Rider *and* Buffalo Bill, Jr. *and* Annie Oakley *to get enough money to buy all his films from Republic. So he owned all of those old Republic movies and owned the ones he made at Columbia. If I'd found out soon enough, I probably could've negotiated with him and bought all the* Buffalo Bill, Jrs.

The Range Rider *and* Buffalo Bill, Jr. *went to public domain right after Autry sold them.*

In the little town of Gene Autry, Oklahoma, a sturdy old schoolhouse has been turned into a fine museum of film cowboy nostalgia. Run by dedicated Elvin Sweeten and his wife, staffed by

*The Gene Autry Oklahoma Museum.*

devoted volunteers and funded by contributions, it is not only a tribute to Gene Autry, but also to the heroes in white hats who rode the silver screen and provided fine role models for a generation of youngsters. It honors the cowboy heroes who taught right from wrong to their fans.

In one room a display pays tribute to Dick Jones and *Buffalo Bill, Jr.* Cases are filled with comics, games, puzzles, decorative plates

and other merchandise inspired by the series, as well as some of Dick's personal memorabilia he gave to the museum, including a gunbelt, shirt and boots.

*I had three gun belts made just for those* [The Range Rider and Buffalo Bill, Jr.] *by Gilmore – with silver. I've got one left. You*

*Memorabilia, including an award plaque.*

*Dick's gunbelt, boots, hat and shirt from Buffalo Bill, Jr. on display.*

*know, if you don't use leather it dies. I've got one like that. The one that was halfway decent I oiled up and put in the Gene Autry, Oklahoma, museum with the shirt and the hat and a pair of boots. There was nothing spectacular about them. I thought Gilmore was the best of anybody around. He did a lot of them. He did Gene's, Roy's [Rogers], the originals.*

It is well worth the trip to wind the back roads from Ardmore, Oklahoma, to go to the Gene Autry Oklahoma Museum and see the memorabilia.

After Dick retired, Western festival organizers were finally able to coax him into appearing at film festivals to meet his fans.
Here are two of the fans' favorite stills for Dick to autograph.

*Fan favorite* Buffalo Bill, Jr. *still.*

*Fan favorite* Buffalo Bill, Jr. *still.*

# *Buffalo Bill, Jr.* Episodes

When asked about specific episodes of *Buffalo Bill, Jr.*, Dick said very few stood out in his memory. "We made two a week. When you go thirteen weeks without stopping, that's twenty-six of them. You lose count."

Episodes of *Buffalo Bill, Jr.*, like those of *The Range Rider*, were not sequenced. They did not build on each other but stood alone. For this reason, other than beginning with "Fight for Geronimo," which has a front title copyright date of 1954 and sets up the premise for the series, the episodes are listed in alphabetical order.

**"Fight for Geronimo"**
Though the episodes for the *Buffalo Bill, Jr.* series have no chronology, this entry was obviously planned to be the first aired. While Judge Wiley often mentions in his show-opening narration that he adopted Buffalo Bill, Jr. and Calamity, he tells a more detailed story to begin "Fight for Geronimo."

Another interesting point is that it is the only episode in which Calamity calls Bill, "Billy." She does this when he attacks Jackilla (Rodd Redwing), thinking that he is hurting Calamity.

When Judge Wiley leaves Bill and Calamity "in jail" to ride to Yuma to alert the troops, the designs on their shirts are explained.

This episode also establishes the fact that Calamity is learning to use the telegraph, something essential to several other episodes.

Many little indicators hint that "Fight for Geronimo" was intended to be the introductory episode.

The plot involves Geronimo (Chief Thundercloud, in one of his last appearances before his death), shown for a short bit of footage, who has been captured by the Army and is being taken by rail to a prison in Florida. The crooked Indian agent, Jed Ford (Harry Lauter) plots his escape in order to tip off the Army to his whereabouts and receive a reward. Bill and Calamity undercover the scheme and set about to thwart the conspiracy.

One of the fun exchanges of the series comes when Bill and Jackilla are talking about the current situation. Bill comments that Geronimo is on the warpath. Jackilla tells him, no, the Army has captured Geronimo, and Bill protests that the telegraph hasn't learned that. Jackilla informs him, "Sometimes white man telegraph not so fast as Indian smoke signals."

As he watches Bill and Calamity ride off, Jackilla smiles and shakes his head with the comment: "White man ways often primitive." Makes me chuckle every time.

Dick agreed this was the first episode:

*I know the one [Buffalo Bill, Jr. episode] they used for the first one. They had Chief Thundercloud in there playing Geronimo. At the very end he's in the railroad car and they had the drapes drawn so they didn't have to have a process camera or a scene behind showing that the train was moving. They just rocked the camera.*

### "Ambush at Lizard Rock"

In "Ambush at Lizard Rock" Wileyville hotel owner, Sy Milford (Syd Saylor), is driving his buckboard near Lizard Rock when he noticed that the old Johnson place is inhabited. He drives up to investigate, startles a little girl into running into the house and is run off by a man with a rifle. He races into Wileyville to tell his story to Judge Wiley.

The Judge and Bill ride out to check out his story. They are greeted by a rifle, too. The Judge tells the man he is the law and demands to know why he is trespassing on the ranch.

Finally the man invites them in, tells them his name is Robert Brown (Stacey Harris) and introduces his daughter Penny (Reba Waters). He says they came from the east and have rented the place. Bill and the Judge know he is hiding something but invite him into town so that Penny can meet Calamity. Then they leave.

After they are gone, Penny cries to her father because she doesn't understand the lying and hiding and running.

Duke Colby (Terry Frost) and his henchman (X Brands) come to Milford's hotel in Wileyville and say they are looking for a friend with a daughter named Penny. Bill, who is walking through the door, becomes immediately suspicious of their aura and manages to stop Milford from blurting out information about the strangers at the Johnson place.

Brown decides to try coming into town. Calamity and Penny have just been introduced when he spots Colby and his henchman and immediately asks the Judge and Bill to take care of Penny, then rushes out of town.

With some clues from Penny, Bill and the Judge learn that Robert Brown is Robert Norman, a witness against a powerful criminal (Colby), who is hiding out until the trial day to stay alive. They make a plan to protect him and put the baddies where they belong – in jail.

### "Angelo Goes West"

Bill and Calamity hear strange music. Following the sound they find Angelo Rosetta (Tito Vicolo) playing his organ to try to entice his monkey Giuseppe down from a tall cactus. He tells them he bought land near Wileyville from a land dealer back East. They recognize it as the old Carson place.

They hear shots and Bill dashes off to investigate. It is a stage holdup. Bill runs off the bandits then goes after the team that ran away when the stage driver (Bob Woodward) was shot and wounded.

Angelo parts with Calamity to go to his new home. The old Carson place is exactly where the outlaws are headed, too. The bandits see Angelo, pull out a badge they took from the marshal they killed and pretend to be lawmen. They tell Angelo they're working un-

*Bill bulldogs two baddies in the "Angelo Goes West" episode.*

dercover and need a place to stay the night.

When Angelo gets up the next morning, they are gone. He checks where they stayed to learn if they will be back that night. When Giuseppe scampers in and finds the badge, he takes it.

The outlaws attack a courier. Bill comes along and gives chase and stops one of them. They are fighting when another of the bandits tries to shoot Bill and kills his own man.

Angelo goes into Wileyville for supplies. While Giuseppe is playing by the cash register, he leaves the badge. That and a telegram about a marshal who was killed tell Bill and the Judge that the killers are close by and must be caught before they catch Angelo up in their scheme and do more damage.

Angelo suspects that the "lawmen" are actually the outlaws but the two that are left force him to help them on their next job.

It's up to Bill to help Angelo and capture the badmen.

## "Apache Raid"

"Apache Raid" starts with Calamity winning a pile of marbles from a friend. These marbles will play a major role later in the story.

Judge Wiley receives a package containing a silver peace pipe for the Mescalero Apache tribe, a gift from the people of Wileyville to honor the years of peace and friendship. He sends Bill out with an invitation to Chief Keetahno (Glenn Strange) to come to town to receive it at a ceremony.

Meanwhile, the Apaches are running a herd belonging to Gorman (Walter Reed) off the reservation. Gorman wants to graze his herd there without paying for grazing rights. The Gorman wranglers chase the Indians and corner Red Wolf (Joseph Michaels). One of the hands draws his gun and fights with Red Wolf over it. The gun fires and the white man is killed. The others corner Red Wolf and start to lynch him. Bill comes along in time to save him, but instead of going to town as Bill told him Red Wolf runs for home.

Gorman comes into the store spouting anti-Indian talk and threatening the Judge. As soon as he leaves, Bill heads for the reservation to talk Red Wolf into coming back to town and to talk with the chief. Keetahno tells Bill of Gorman's illegal activities.

Reluctantly, the Apaches agree to work with Bill and the Judge to find evidence of Gorman's wrongdoings and settle the conflict peacefully.

## "The Assassins"

Ambushers attack Marshal Clint Early (Edgar Dearing). Bill comes along in time to take him to town. Before he dies, he tells them they must get to San Josita before the afternoon stage. He and Mexican lawman Ramon Chevez (Rico Alaniz) have been working together to catch smugglers. Both their lives were threatened and the assassins will try for Chevez when he arrives in San Josita. Early says to tell his son Jeff (Mike Garrett) it's up to him now.

Judge Wiley and Bill start immediately in time to get there before the arrival of the stage.

Jeff is known around town as a playboy and gambler but hearing of the death of his father makes him determined to be a good lawman. His first step, after deputizing Bill and the Judge, is to outlaw guns in town. The three of them then start a circuit of the town, gathering all the guns.

C.L. Morgan (Michael Bryant), a mild-looking ladies wear salesman who has a stiff leg and walks with a cane, watches as Bill and a man the audience knows as one of the assassins fight. After the fight, he congratulates Bill on his good fighting and says he wishes guns could be outlawed in every town. He carries only a derringer for personal protection and willingly gives it up.

As he walks to the hotel he speaks to the man Bill left lying in the street.

When Morgan gets to his hotel room his henchmen are waiting. The boss carefully stretches out his stiff leg and removes the rifle that is strapped to it. Then he pulls the short guns from his other leg. His hotel window faces the stage depot and here comes the stage with the Mexican lawman.

It's Calamity, who followed them to San Josita, who sees the killer and alerts Bill to prevent the assassination.

### "The Black Ghost"

Calamity's feminine intuition and Fourth of July firecrackers are key factors in "The Black Ghost." It is one of the episodes that features Bill's little sister.

Judge Wiley gets a letter from his old friend, Bob Barton (Ewing Mitchell), that says he's returning to his ranch outside of Wileyville with his niece Alice (Claudia Barrett). Bill and Calamity go out to the ranch to welcome them but are met with hostility by a man (Denver Pyle) who tells them he's the foreman. Bill challenges him over the broken lock on the door and they fight. The "foreman" gives Bill an explanation after the fight.

As Bill and Calamity start for home they hear gunshots and rush to the road to find that the Black Ghost (Bill Henry) is attacking the buckboard carrying Barton and his niece. Barton is injured and they take him to Wileyville. Bill tells Alice, whom he describes as "brave," that the Black Ghost is a dangerous outlaw but has not been around Wileyville before.

One look at Alice and Bill is head over heels in love. The Judge is also smitten.

Alice asks for her uncle's papers and says she wants to go to the ranch to be alone. Such a brave girl. The Judge gives her everything but what appears to be the will, a sealed envelope with the Judge's name on it to be opened at Barton's death.

At the ranch Alice joins her lover, the Black Ghost, and tells him the will is still with the Judge.

With Bill and the Judge both taken in by the lovely, brave Alice, it's up to Calamity to reveal the truth and save the day.

### "Blazing Guns"

"Blazing Guns" opens with two men robbing Henry Martin (Edgar Dearing) practically at the edge of Wileyville.

Shift to the general store where the Judge is giving a boy a haircut. Martin bursts in and accuses the Judge of not doing anything about the robberies that have been taking place. Barnaby Darrow (Gayne Whitman) defends his efforts.

After everyone else leaves, Bill, Judge Wiley and Calamity puzzle over how the robbers find out who is carrying money.

Shift again to the dress shop of Craig Hollister (Kirk Alyn) where the robbers, Slick (Stacey Harris) and Tony (Dennis Moore) bring him the money they have just stolen from Martin. Tony suggests moving on but Hollister insists there is more money in the area to be had.

Calamity goes to the dress shop to get Hollister to help her with the dress she is sewing and, while she's in back putting on the dress, hears Helen Darrow (Helen Brown) ordering dresses and telling Hollister that for the first time she doesn't have to worry about money. Then she proceeds to tell him her husband's plan for getting his cash past the bandits.

When Darrow is held up and wounded, he turns on the Judge.

After he storms out, Bill comments that no one knew of Darrow's plan. Calamity pipes up, "I knew it," and tells about overhearing Mrs. Darrow confiding the plan to Hollister. Aha! The dressmaker knew, too.

Later Calamity bumps into Slick looking into the window at the dress shop.

When Bill talks to all those who have been robbed, he learns that every one has a relative who had recently ordered from and visited with the dressmaker.

Bill, Calamity and the Judge decide to set a trap for Hollister and prove that Judge Wiley is still a good marshal.

### "Boomer's Blunder"

In "Boomer's Blunder" Judge Wiley and his friend, Caleb Boomer (Stanley Andrews), are still fighting the War Between the States, although in reality they have been friends for many years.

When Caleb was in need of money, the Judge bought some of his land. Now Boomer wants it back. Actually, he needs to get it back.

Bellamy (Don C. Harvey) has told Caleb he will give him a good price for some of his land but only if it includes the acres that the Judge bought. The land contains tungsten ore and at this point Bellamy and his henchmen are the only ones who know.

When the Judge refuses to sell, Bellamy sends one of his henchmen, John-O (Lee Van Cleef) back into the store with Boomer to insist the sale is made.

In a store-wrecking fight Bill and John-O knock each other winding until the last blow when John-O ends up covered with flour.

Bill and Calamity follow Caleb home and learn about Bellamy's proposition. Bill becomes suspicious and investigates with Calamity's help – something rare, as Bill usually tried to make her stay home.

### "A Bronc Called Gunboat"

Bill and Calamity have scrimped and saved to order a special gift for Judge Wiley for his birthday, briar pipes from England. After surprising him with a cake and helping to blow out all the candles, Bill rides out to meet the stage and get the package from the mailbag.

Marshal Benton Early (Harry Lauter) and his prisoner Blackjack Johnson (George J. Lewis) are among the passengers. Two men attack the stage and Bill transfers to his horse to chase them. In the process, he knocks the package from England out the stage door and the pipes are crushed. It will take $24 to replace them.

The marshal asks the Judge if he has jail space to hold Johnson until the train going their way arrives in a few days. He says he needs some guards because Blackjack has friends still on the outside. The Judge says they will round up some help.

*Bill makes a flying leap to stop a villain in "Boomer's Blunder."*

A dejected Bill and Calamity are trying to figure out how they will replace the pipes when the entry parade for Colonel Shaw's Rodeo comes down the street. The Colonel (Stanley Andrews) introduces Gunboat, the champion bronc who has never been ridden, then Clay Holder (Eddie Dew), the greatest bronc rider, who will try to ride Gunboat the next day. Bill doesn't perk up until he hears that the bronc riding is open and anyone who stays on Gunboat for ten seconds will win $25, one more dollar than he and Calamity need.

The Colonel and Holder are reluctant to let Bill sign up because of his age and inexperience but he finally talks them into it.

Holder goes first and this time breaks his leg when Gunboat throws him. Bill, too, is thrown two seconds before he could win the money. He's feeling like a real loser until Holder gives him a lecture/pep talk, telling him the measure of a man is not only how he wins but how he loses.

Shaw has a new idea to bring in crowds. Now he plans to shoot Gunboat in the rodeo arena the next day at noon, calling him a killer when actually he just broke Holder's leg. Clay protests, as do Bill, Calamity and the Judge, but Gunboat is the Colonel's property and in the Old West he could do as he pleased.

Blackjack's friends decide the best time to break him from jail will be when the horse is shot. They overpower the marshal and Johnson escapes.

Bill and Holder have worked out a plan to save Gunboat but it will take interaction between the horse and the outlaws before Shaw is convinced just how valuable Gunboat is.

### "The Calico Kid"

Sagebrush Smith (Hank Patterson) is so depressed over his troubles that he tries to pick a gunfight with noted gunfighter Tom Stace (Lee Van Cleef) in hopes that he'll be shot.

It seems that the old prospector's daughter Penelope (Mollie McCart) is coming west to see him. All these years he's lied to her in letters saying he's a prosperous man from his rich gold mine.

Bill and the Judge clean him up so that he looks well-off but his next problem is that he's told her how wild the area is. Bill decides to help him out on that front by pretending to be the Calico Kid and holding up the stage on which Penelope travels.

As is ever true, such a masquerade can only lead to disaster, as the Wileyville people pile lie upon lie to protect Penelope from the knowledge of her father's real situation.

The best description of "The Calico Kid" is the famous quote, "Oh, what a tangled web we weave ..."

### "Constance and the Judge" aka "The Lady and the Judge"

Mrs. Constance Hamilton (Louise Lorimer), a widow from Massachusetts, gets off the stage at Wileyville and asks for the real estate office. As the town has none, Bill takes her to Judge Wiley, who holds most of the town offices.

She tells the Judge she's been restless since being widowed and she decided to relocate to the West. The Judge is delighted to drive her out to look at property. Two masked men stop them and take the Judge's wallet and Constance's handbag, which supposedly

*Dick and an unidentified stuntman fight in "Constance and the Judge."*

*Dick catches on the rail to pull himself back up to continue the fight in "Constance and the Judge."*

contains $10,000. Bill chases the thieves but catches the one who is not carrying the money.

Since her money has been stolen, the Judge invites Constance to stay with them.

In the night Bill hears a noise and investigates. Calamity is in her bed but Constance is not. Bill goes outside and catches the prisoner escaping. He is knocked out. When he comes to and goes back to check on Calamity, their visitor is asleep in her bed.

Mrs. Hamilton's attorney and business manager, George Hanford (Rick Vallin) arrives on the stage. The minute they are alone, she tells him she wants to call this off. These are good people. Hanford brushes her off, saying if she refuses to cooperate in the scheme he will make sure her brother goes to jail. Constance is torn between her brother and her new friends in Wileyville.

Bill doesn't like the way things have been going since the lady arrived. First the holdup, then the prisoner escaping by using a passkey, now her attorney arriving from Boston while wearing a coat bought at a store west of Wileyville.

He and Calamity have their own dilemma. Believing that the Judge is in love with Constance, do they break his heart now or wait to see if Constance is involved in the questionable activities?

This script was written by Maurice Geraghty. His experience in screenwriting contributes to making it a fine episode.

### "The Death of Johnny Ringo"

Many believe "The Death of Johnny Ringo" episode was the pilot for the *Buffalo Bill, Jr.* series. It was obviously an early episode but it does not set up the premise for the series as "Fight for Geronimo" does. The front title also has a 1955 copyright date while "Fight for Geronimo" shows 1954.

In this episode Jack Deuce, masquerading as Johnny Ringo (George J. Lewis), steals bonds that belong to the Piute tribe and the Army must retrieve them quickly in order to avoid war. Bill is shot at by Ringo and reports it.

Hearing the name, Buffalo Bill, Jr., Captain Corey Heath (Harry Lauter) believes he must be a fine tracker and calls upon Bill to help him track the outlaw down. There's a lesson here in not pretending to be what you are not. However, Bill tracking skills are sufficient to get the job done.

Meanwhile, back in the Wileyville, Anna Louise Beaumont (Angie Dickinson) appears at the door seeking Johnny Ringo. Then Larry Martin (James Best), Calamity's telegrapher friend who is bringing the telegram from Heath to Bill, is shot and wounded on their doorstep.

This storyline is complex and packed with good action. At one point Captain Heath asks Bill, "Don't you ever mount or dismount the regular way?" Bill replies, "Yes, sir. When I have lots of time."

Dick could not confirm that "The Death of Johnny Ringo" was the pilot episode, but the presence of Angie Dickinson and James Best in their only appearances in the series would indicate that it was not made using the standard two-episodes-made-at-the-same-time-with-the-same-cast scheduling. That is the only fact that makes this episode stand out in any way as a possible pilot. It does not confirm it, as several other actors and actresses are seen only once, including Buzz Henry and Chuck Courtney.

### "The Devil's Washbowl"

All of Wileyville is buzzing about the stranger who has come to town. Jonathan Quimby (Myron Healey) rides out into the desert every day without explanation and sends nonsense telegrams such as: "Blueberry muffins. Sour cream. Fiddle-dee-dee. STOP. Don't let blackbird out of pie." They all go to Miss Florence Pike, Frontier Hotel, Kansas City.

When Quimby has them all neatly hooked, he tells the townsfolk that the water of the Devil's Washbowl, a bubbling, smelly pool out from town, is healing and he's bought the land around it. Miss Pike (Grace Field) will be in on the stage with $50,000 to build a hotel. The Devil's Washbowl will become a major luxury spa, a profitable boom for Wileyville.

The stage is held up, but not really, the robbers are working with Quimby and Pike.

The people of the town send out searchers but by the fourth day it looks like the bandits have escaped. Miss Pike and Quimby tell Judge Wiley they are leaving for the East to raise more money but

*Bill is jerked from his horse in "The Devil's Washbowl."*

the Judge, dreaming of Wileyville becoming a major health resort, suggests that they try to raise the money locally first.

The whole town jumps on the bandwagon except for skeptical Bill. He doubts the merits of such a stinky pool. Then, when Calamity mentions to him that her Indian friend says that the Devil's Washbowl is bad medicine, he knows something is wrong and starts to seek the truth. He even takes Calamity along to help him.

### "Diamonds for Grandpa"

Grandpa Andrews (William Fawcett) is the Wileyville town character. He takes good care of his grandson Sonny (Brad Morrow), but periodically roars into town proclaiming he's found gold or silver or another ore.

Julia Slade (Renee Godfrey) comes to Wileyville from the District Welfare Agency to talk to Judge Wiley. She is investigating Andrews because the agency doesn't believe he's fit to raise Sonny. [Was there any child welfare office on the frontier?] The Judge tells her Sonny has a good home. Grandpa is just a little eccentric.

Unfortunately, Grandpa picks this moment to rush into town shouting he's found a diamond strike. His exuberant celebration convinces Slade he's too incompetent to raise a child and the Judge doesn't help with his efforts to calm Grandpa down. The old man unholsters his gun and he and the boy back out of the store to go stake his claim.

Mase Dillon (George J. Lewis) and his two henchmen, Spud (James Seay) and Kansas (Slim Pickens) hear Andrews raising a ruckus and believe that he has struck it rich.

When Grandpa and Sonny leave town, Dillon sends his rowdies after them and goes into the store for more information. He casually asks about the supposed strike. The Judge scorns the idea but Calamity shows him the rough rock Grandpa gave her. It's her very own diamond.

Bill and Calamity, on the way to the dentist, come upon Spud and Kansas waylaying Andrews and Sonny. Before Bill can run them off, Grandpa tells the outlaws he has gold, too, making the baddies think he is crazy, especially when they see the rough rocks he calls diamonds. Bill chases the robbers off, but not before they have given Andrews a serious crack on the head.

When his henchmen arrive at the shack, Dillon demands the map for the claim. They tell him the old man's crazy. No diamonds. Dillon is furious. He was once a diamond smuggler. He knows what the rocks will reveal when properly processed.

With Grandpa in bed, Julia moves into the house to prepare to take Sonny away. As the Judge leaves after doctoring Andrews, he tells her he will fight her tooth and nail to keep her from taking the boy. When she tells him he'll lose, he retorts that at least he'll know he's acted like a human being.

Meanwhile, Calamity has been doing some research and has learned that there are diamond mines in America. She and Bill go to Mr. Goren (Mauritz Hugo), who has spent time in Brazil, and he confirms that Calamity's rock is indeed a diamond.

Now Bill has to convince Julia not to take Sonny, as well as prevent the crooks from stealing Grandpa's wealth.

### "Double-Cross Money"

The Blue River Bank desperately needs a money shipment. Two masked men stop the courier bringing the cash and steal the strongbox.

*Bill stops a team that has run away with Calamity in "Empire Pass."*

Longtime Granite City Bank employee Henry Cameron (Stanley Andrews) wants the bank to operate for the good of the community. The former owner's nephew Ned Ranton (Rick Vallin), who inherited the bank, wants to run it strictly for-profit, squeezing every drop from the townsfolk.

Cameron protests that the younger man's ways are causing people to move their accounts to the Blue River Bank. Ned says that bank won't be a consideration for long.

Ranton sends the old employee on a long-delayed vacation, insisting that he works too hard, then goes into the back room to meet with one of the bandits who just stole the cash intended for Blue River. As for a place to hide it? Ned points out that only he and Cameron know the combination to the vault and he just sent the old man on a vacation. What safer place could there be than in a bank vault?

Cameron stops by Wileyville on his way and finds a group of citizens discussing the imminent closure of the Blue River Bank and the possibility of Wileyville starting a bank of its own.

Henry asks Judge Wiley for twenty-four hours to talk Ned into changing the Granite City Bank policies before the people of Wileyville take steps to form their own bank and the Judge agrees. Cameron leaves the store to go back to Granite City.

Calamity is trying to play matchmaker between Henry and Ellen Forthergill (Louise Lorimer) and is happy to drive Miss Ellen to Granite City to close out her account there to get money for the Wileyville bank.

When Cameron goes to the vault to get Miss Ellen's money, he discovers the extra cash from the robbery. Ned's henchman sees the old man in the vault and tells his boss. They decide they must kill him before he can tell Judge Wiley about the money.

Bill is on his way to Granite City at the time the murder attempt is made and takes Cameron to Wileyville. Cameron tells the Judge about the extra money in the vault. The Judge has the serial numbers of the bills that were stolen. If they could find a way to see the extra money in the Granite City bank, they would know if there was a connection to the robbery.

With all the disturbance, Ellen had forgotten the money she got when she closed her account. The serial numbers match. Bill and the Judge devise a plan to trap Ned Ranton and his henchmen and get the money to its rightful owner, the Blue River Bank.

### "Empire Pass"

Keeping a railroad connection to Wileyville is the challenge in "Empire Pass."

Rocky Mountain and Southern Railroad superintendent McKeever (Bill Kennedy) comes to Wileyville with bad news. The Continental Pacific Railroad is planning to lay rails through Empire Pass, which will put the Rocky Mountain and Southern out of business and leave Wileyville stranded one hundred miles from a rail connection.

The Rocky Mountain and Southern could pay for the rails to be competitive for the line through the pass but labor costs are beyond its means. Bill suggests that the people of Wileyville may be willing to do the labor for free if it means keeping a rail connection.

*Buffalo Bill, Jr. poses with a Texas flag.*

As the townsmen are making plans, two men, Toad (Mike Ragan) and Kilgore (Terry Frost) come into the store and start a ruckus. Turns out they are henchmen for Dunlap (Mauritz Hugo), who works for the Continental Pacific and will do anything to beat out the competition.

Dunlap and his henchmen can't get rails onsite to head off Bill's plan for the Rocky Mountain and Southern, but they can fake it. Bill and Calamity learn of the scheme and work all night to thwart the other railroad's charade and save the rail connection to Wileyville.

## "The Fight for Texas"

As Judge Ben Wiley tells us in his narration that begins the episode, this is a story of the Texas Rangers.

Captain Kenneth McNabb (Steve Pendleton) rides into Wileyville seeking a telegraph station. Calamity sends him to Wileyville Junction where Bill is waiting for the mail to arrive. The telegrapher has been called away but Bill goes for Calamity to send the urgent message for the captain. He is asking permission to cross the Rio Grande in pursuit of bandits.

J.L. Jeffers (Tom Keene as Richard Powers) comes in on the mail train. He and McNabb have a confrontation over his lack of support for the Rangers. Nevertheless, Jeffers offers McNabb the use of his private telegraph, which will save an hour if the Rangers receive permission to cross the river after the rustlers.

But Jeffers has ulterior motives. He wants the Rangers to cross illegally to cause an international incident and discredit McNabb, which just might put the Rangers out of business.

Bill and Calamity learn of the plot and hurry to stop the crossing and save the Rangers but Bill does not arrive in time. Now Bill must work to devise a Plan B to restore McNabb and the Rangers to their former glory.

## "First Posse"

The historical characters in "First Posse" are Wyatt Earp (Walter Reed), Doc Holliday (James Griffith) and Frank Stillwell (Lane Bradford).

Stillwell enters the Wileyville store with a wounded gang member (Bob Woodward) and holds Judge Wiley and Bill at gunpoint, demanding that the Judge tend the wound. Calamity comes from behind Stillwell and hits him over the head. He and Bill are fighting when Earp and Holliday come in and capture Stillwell.

After locking Stillwell and his buddy in the Wileyville jail, the Arizona lawmen share a meal with the family before hitting the road with their prisoners. Talk turns to posses. Bill expresses his strong desire to ride with one but is quickly shot down by the Judge and the law officers because he is young.

The Arizona men leave with their prisoners but soon Holliday is

*In "First Posse," Bill must borrow a horse to chase Calamity's runaway.*

back. Stillwell has escaped and Holliday needs to enlist a posse to track him down.

Crushed, Bill saddles up, still determined to tag along. Calamity tags right after him, necessitating Bill's return to Wileyville just in time to land smack in the middle of the action. Stillwell has also returned to Wileyville to take revenge on the Judge for helping in his capture. Bill and Calamity arrive in the nick of time.

### "Fugitive from Injustice"

At the beginning of "Fugitive from Injustice," Bill and Calamity are out for Bill's target practice when Bill spies a rifle sighted at them. Just as quickly the rifle disappears. Bill follows the track to a deserted ranch. Then the rifle is pointed at them from behind the shack door.

Bill calls out and a young boy, Pepito Gonzales (Peter Votrian), emerges gun in hand and tells them to leave. Bill surmises that the youngster is in trouble and rides away with the plan to return with food to entice the boy to tell them what is wrong. He notes to Calamity that from the ground signs he has read, the kid is alone with a mare and a foal.

After they ride away, Pepito goes to the barn to saddle the mare,

Chiquita. Two outlaws (Harry Lauter and Eddie Parker) riding double see the child struggling to take a saddle off the fence and decide their need for a second horse will quickly be fulfilled. They accost Pepito and take Chiquita, leaving him with the colt, Etanito.

The bandits see Tinker (Hank Patterson) putting up a wanted poster. As soon as he is out of sight, they ride over to see if it is about them but discover it's for Pepito, a reward put on his head by Otis McComb (Henry Rowland) accusing him of stealing the horses.

Deciding they can use the $1000 reward, they follow Tinker and tell him his job of posting the notices is done.

As Bill and Calamity return to the ranch with food, they encounter Pepito leading Etanito along the road. The food weakens his resistance and he is eating when the outlaws return to take the colt. Bill chases them off but stops to help Tinker when he gets in the way. They all go to Wileyville.

Bill and Judge Wiley would like some answers to this puzzle but Tinker can't read so he can't tell them about the wanted posters and Pepito won't talk. Finally Tinker remembers he used a poster to line his leaky boot. Now the Judge and Bill know about McComb's claim. Pepito swears to them the horses are his. Then Bill finds a bill of sale for the horses in Pepito's hat, which shows that he does own the horses.

It's up to the Judge to determine whose claims represent the truth and see that the rightful owner keeps the horses.

### "The Golden Plant"

When Wang Chin (Keye Luke) buys the worthless Soledad mine from Garson (House Peters, Jr.), his granddaughter's fiancé Ah Lee (Billy Lee) claims he has stolen the money Min Toy (Barbara Jean Wong) sent for their wedding.

Garson and Melvin Jessup (Walter Reed) are swindlers who sell and resell the worthless mine to gullible buyers.

But Wang Chin is a clever buyer. When the supplies for the Chinese wedding – firecrackers, lanterns, spinners and other explosives – come in, Calamity takes them to the mine and finds Chin digging, but not for gold. Ginseng grows wild at the Soledad mine site and the old man knows its value.

Calamity helps him prepare the crop to be shipped and he tells her to put the wedding supplies in the bunkhouse.

When Jessup discovers that Wang Chin is reaping a rich reward for what he's digging up at the mine, he is furious. For the first shipment alone, Chin was paid $8000. Jessup tells him he'll be charged with fraud if he knew about the ginseng when he bought the land but Wang Chin is unruffled.

The old man insists that Ah Lee accompany him to the mine and sends the boy out to the hillside to find the riches so valued by the Chinese. Then he goes into his shack where Garson and Jessup are waiting for him. Garson kills him and they take the thousands.

When Ah Lee hears the shot, he runs for the shack in time to be hit on the head and left beside Wang Chin with a gun.

Because they had argued, the Judge believes Ah Lee is the killer but Bill thinks he is innocent. Bill and Calamity convince the Judge to let them prove it and come up with a plan to expose the true villains.

### "Grave of the Monsters"

In his show-introducing narration, Judge Wiley tells that the Navajo reservation is not far from Wileyville. On it is a bubbling tar pit called the Grave of the Monsters. A shrine has been built there to the monster god.

White Eagle (Joseph Michaels), son of Chief Black Elk (Glenn Strange), and Bill are so close that the Judge wonders if Bill is part Navajo.

White Eagle and Bill meet at the shrine. Bill is on his way to deliver supplies to the Indian village and White Eagle is waiting to meet the Indian agent, Jim Bartlett (Fred Libby), who wants the young Indian to show him where he saw strangers on the reservation.

White Eagle takes Bartlett to the place and they see three men surveying the area. Bartlett rides down to confront them.

The head man, Dr. Paul Haddon (Walter Reed), introduces himself as a naturalist and his assistant in surveying, Bert Major (Tom Monroe). He tells the agent they are checking the survey before filing a claim. Bartlett tells them they are on Indian land and he was on the original survey team. There is no error. Major kills him and they drop him into the tar pit.

White Eagle watches this from the rocks on the ridge. The men spy him and give chase. One of the henchmen (Bob Woodward) knocks White Eagle out and shoves him down a sharp incline just as Bill comes along in time to save him.

After White Eagle has been rescued, Bill goes home to find Judge Wiley trying out his new dental tools on Calamity. Bill suggests that the Judge needs to advertise and says he saw something on the reservation that would be perfect.

He and Calamity head for the Indian land to bring back the big, ancient tooth Bill saw near the Grave of the Monsters. In addition to the tooth, Bill finds the survey notebook that Major had lost. He sends the tooth back to Wileyville with Calamity.

Meanwhile, Major has discovered the loss and has come back to look for his notebook. He and Bill fight and he throws Bill into the tar pit. White Eagle arrives at the shrine in time to save Bill and now has the chance to tell him about the murder he witnessed.

In town, Haddon has come to the Judge to file his falsified claim with its doctored information. He sees the tooth that Calamity has brought into town and asks about it. Calamity tells him the tooth came from the reservation and how close she is to White Eagle. Under the subterfuge of having her show him exactly where she found the tooth, Haddon kidnaps her.

Now Bill must save Calamity in the process of capturing the killers.

## "Gun Talk"

Gary Holden (Harry Lauter) and his son Lance (Barry Curtis) live out from Wileyville. They are in town to check on Lance's horse, Charger, who has been severely ill and is being treated by Judge Wiley.

While they are in town, the express office is robbed. Holden shoots down one of the robbers before he can shoot Bill in the back but the other two escape. Bill goes after them and manages to make them drop the express bag but does not catch either one.

Gary agrees to go with Bill the next morning to track them.

What Gary does not know is that the bandit leader, Shanghai (Lane Bradford), recognized him as Jerry McOwen from the days when he rode the outlaw trail and is waiting in his barn to get help for his wound and take a horse to escape.

Holden agrees to get him bandages and food and leave a horse behind the barn for Shanghai. The villain wants Charger but Holden tells him the horse is his son's and is sick. To ride him will kill him.

The next morning Bill and Calamity go out to the ranch for Bill to pick up Gary to track with him and for Calamity to spend the day with Lance. When the kids go out with Charger's medicine, the horse is gone.

The four of them start following those tracks and find Charger dead. Lance is devastated and his father is killing mad.

Gary shows up at the store, says he has to make a trip and asks the Judge to look after Lance while he's gone. The Judge is suspicious and believes, rightly, that Holden is going after the man who killed his son's horse. What he doesn't know is that the two men once rode together.

The Judge sends Bill after Holden. Bill doesn't know what to make of it when he ends up at the outlaws' hideout. Gary must prove to Bill that he has gone straight and help capture the outlaw gang.

### "Hooded Vengeance"

In "Hooded Vengeance" it's the Ku Klux Klan menacing the area around Wileyville.

Calamity sees the Klan attacking the ranch of the Claytons, Ben (Bill Henry) and Martha (Claudia Barrett).

Ben is fighting a Klansman in the living room when the attacker's hood catches fire and he yanks is from his head. The Claytons see his face.

Meanwhile, Calamity runs to tell Bill, who is talking with a townsman, Tracy (Ewing Mitchell), who advises against challenging the Klan. Bill preaches him a sermon on the importance of law-abiding people being willing to stand up against the wrong rather than be intimidated, then rides for the Clayton property.

When he arrives, they refuse to even admit the Klan was there even though Calamity saw them. Ben says they are pulling up stakes and leaving the area. Martha protests but Ben's mind is made up.

Despite the Claytons' denial of a raid, Bill follows the tracks that lead from the house until he and Calamity are far out of town. Only one ranch is farther down the road, the Duncan place. Calamity shudders and says he killed a man but still insists on going with Bill, who plans to check out that ranch. Just as they are in the barn examining a horse that had recently been ridden hard, Duncan (Dennis Moore) comes in. He and Bill fight and Bill and Calamity escape.

When Clayton goes to see the real estate man, Delafield (Denver Pyle), to get back the money he has paid down on his ranch, Delafield tells him the money is not returnable. Ben protests that he was told he could have his money if he left but Delafield replies that offer was only good for thirty days.

Clayton demands that they take this issue to Judge Wiley, who reads the contract and rules that it is legally binding.

Bill and Calamity return and Bill asks the Judge if Clayton told him about the raid. The Judge says no, Clayton repeats that they are moving and the Judge says that it seems like every time good people try to settle, the Klan runs them off.

Judge Wiley offers to forget all that Clayton owes the store if they will try to stick it out a little longer. He can't refuse that offer and they devise a plan to try to capture the Klan members.

To start it off, Clayton tells Delafield he's changed his mind and won't be leaving. Delafield does not get the property back. Then Bill convinces some of the townsmen to join the enterprise.

Things don't go as smoothly as hoped but all the hitches produce some fine action-packed scenes, making "Hooded Vengeance" a good episode for action-lovers.

Dick remembered that particular episode.

*The outlaws caught us* [Bill and Calamity] *and we hid in the barn. We put on their costumes. I kept having to grab her hood and pull it up so she would look taller. We went charging out of the barn and she kept getting tangled up in her costume, so I just grabbed her by her belt and threw her up on the back of the horse and we chased off.*

## "The Jayhawker"

The Jayhawker (Michael Bryant) is another vicious outlaw. He leaves a trail of destruction in his path. But he's no match for Buffalo Bill, Jr.

When he and his henchman Matt (Gregg Barton) rob the bank in Sand Creek, Judge Wiley sends Bill after them. As they are being pursued, the outlaws hide the saddlebags holding their loot in the rocks.

Young Danny (Lee Erickson) sees them and takes the saddlebags.

After Bill captures the Jayhawker, the Judge goes to Sand Creek to preside over the trial. Bill and Calamity go, too. As they reach town, someone runs from the general store, jumps on a horse and hightails it down the street. The store owner runs out shouting that he's been robbed. Bill takes off after the thief, who turns out to be fifteen-year-old Danny.

Danny is one of the Reverend's boys in a home/school in the town. He's the black sheep of the bunch. The Reverend Jeff Masters (Mike Garrett) is former Kansas gunman, Jeff Kincaid, who has changed his name and his way of life to help boys follow the good path.

From his cell, the Jayhawker sees the Reverend through the bars and remembers him from Abilene.

Matt comes to break out the Jayhawker as Calamity and Danny bring his food. Danny tells the outlaws that he has stolen their ill-gotten gains and offers to trade the loot for the chance to ride the outlaw trail with them. The Jayhawker will agree to anything to get the money and has Danny lead them to the stash, which is hidden in the school barn.

Bill, the Judge and the Reverend go after them, with the Reverend intent on proving to Danny that the way he teaches is best and Bill intent on returning the Jayhawker to jail.

## "Kansas City Lady"

Tim Dobson's (Brad Morrow) father has been gone for a month, the longest trip he's taken since Tim's mother died. Now he's coming home with a big surprise. Tim is hoping for a pony but it turns out to be a new stepmother, Linda (Renee Godfrey). To say Tim is not happy would be a gross understatement.

While they are visiting by the store, a fight breaks out in the street. Bill starts to stop it but realizes it is a diversion when he sees Joe (Bob Woodward) slink toward the bank door. Bill goes after Joe, leaving the Judge to handle the ruckus in the street.

The man who started the fight is Dude Simpson (Slim Pickens), who quickly points out there is no proof to tie him to the robbery attempt. He's allowed to leave town but not before he sees a familiar face, Linda Dobson, formerly known as Linda Abbott.

Dude and Joe decide they need to notify Monte Lassiter (George J. Lewis). He would like to know where Linda is and that she is married to the owner of a stage line. As stage owner, Mark Dobson (James Seay) receives a list of dates on which payrolls ship. That could be very interesting to Lassiter.

When Monte appears at her door, Linda is shocked and angry. Lassiter tries to blackmail her into helping him learn about money shipments but she throws him out. He leaves, but not before he sees the list of payroll ship dates on Mark's desk.

The stages carrying payrolls begin to be stopped, *only* those that are carrying payroll. Someone must be tipping off the bandits.

Bill and Dobson plan a trap and catch Dude. He won't talk but the stage driver describes Monte Lassiter and Tim pipes up that it sounds like the man who visited his stepmother, but he doesn't tell everything he heard.

Linda admits she knew Lassiter in Kansas City but swears she has nothing to do with the robberies. The banker wants an investigation. Dobson assures the Judge that Linda will be there when they want her so he lets her go home.

Calamity and Tim are playing at his house when they see Linda, carrying a gun, get on her pony and ride toward Mesquite Canyon. Calamity, who has stood up for Linda from the first, runs for Bill to get him on her trail to protect her either from whatever trouble she might encounter – or from herself.

## "Kid Curry – Killer"

Now Harvey Logan, Kid Curry (Walter Reed), is the most vicious killer of the Old West. AND – he's threatening Wileyville.

Action starts with Jackilla (Rodd Redwing) waking Bill in the night to tell him that he saw a marshal shot. When Bill and Jackilla get to the site they find a note pinned on the body saying, "He crowded me. I don't like being crowded. Kid Curry."

Calamity has followed them. Bill sends her back to tell Judge Wiley and telegraph notice of the marshal's death.

Joe Hill (House Peters, Jr.) comes into the store as the Judge is pinning on his marshal's badge to step into that role. The Judge tells Hill he is after Kid Curry. Then Bill comes in to say the tracks showed that Curry had two men with him and the Judge decides they need a posse.

Hill says that it won't be easy to get men to go up against the Kid and gives them a speech filled with homage to Kid Curry.

Before they can organize a posse, the Kid and his henchmen blow up a train and steal $62,000. Calamity rushes in to get the Judge for his doctor capacity. Many were injured or killed in the explosion.

Calamity and the Judge come back from the wreck site with Tommy Howard (Louis Lettieri), the marshal's son, who was on the train and was injured.

Meanwhile, Kid Curry is low on ammunition and comes into Wileyville to get it. Bill is on the way to the gunsmith to pick up his gun that had jammed and recognizes the Kid. They fight, but the outlaw gets away and the small posse of Bill, Jackilla, Hill and the Judge set out after him.

Hill's actions arouse the suspicions of the others and the Judge decides to use Hill to lead them to Kid Curry.

### "Legacy of Jesse James"

Rancher John Gilford (Bob Woodward) is murdered. His hired man Bert Corey (Buzz Henry) is suspected. Corey runs; Bill goes after him.

With prisoner in tow, Bill is headed back to Wileyville when he meets Bob Kent (House Peters, Jr.) on the road. Kent asks where he can find John Gilford. Bill says he was killed. Hearing that, Kent says he has a tale to tell that might indicate Corey is innocent. Bill suggests they go to Wileyville and tell it to the Judge.

There Kent proceeds to relate a story of the "Legacy of Jesse James." Kent says he and two other men, John Gilford and Max McCreary (Carleton Young), rode with James as a part of Quantrill's Raiders. After the four broke away, the other three learned that Jesse had buried a quarter of a million in cash. The other three insisted he share and a map was drawn which was torn into four pieces. Each man took a piece.

After James was killed, the other two learned that McCreary had gotten Jesse's piece of the map. Now McCreary has been released from prison and Gilford has been killed. Kent thinks McCreary is the murderer.

McCreary has already hit the area with violence, stealing horses from the Indians and taking supplies from Cass Ricketts' store.

The Judge still holds Corey and remands him to the county seat. He takes Kent into protective custody as a material witness and the next morning they all head out.

The journey is long and as the day draws toward an end, Bill sees the tracks of an Indian pony in their path. He suggests for more protection from an Indian attack they sidetrack for the night to a shack by Potter's Lake.

Guess what landmark is on Kent's piece of the map. It will all come to a head here after Corey escapes and ends up in McCreary hands.

### "The Little Mavericks"

"The Little Mavericks" is one of the episodes that features Calamity.

Now it's one of the Youngers menacing the Wileyville area. Bill brings in wanted posters for Ace Younger (House Peters, Jr.) and his partner Kansas (Carleton Young). Calamity says that the $1000 reward would be worth the effort to try and find out the location of the outlaws. After all, it's for *information* leading to their capture. She wouldn't have to actually capture them.

Bill and the Judge firmly tell her that job is not for little girls and shoo her away but do let her take one of the posters to put on her clubhouse wall.

Calamity has a need for the money. She and her friends have formed a club. They call themselves the Mavericks. The sister of her best friend in the club, Ellen Tyler (Frances Karath), needs expensive surgery to walk again. When Bertha (Sharon Baird) can walk again, she can be in the club, too.

At the club meeting, Calamity proposes that the girls look for information on the outlaws in order to get money for Bertha's operation. They are looking only for information, she cautions them. [Calamity being cautious? Quite a surprise for fans.] If they find something suspicious, they will report it to Bill at once. They will ride in pairs for safety.

Partners Calamity and Ellen have been out all day with no luck when they spot the old, deserted Johnson place. Calamity says they should check it out, then go home.

Jackpot! They find evidence the men are staying there and start to run for their horses to go get Bill.

Their way is blocked. Ace and Kansas are riding up to the barn.

Now they have the information they need but they are trapped. Surely when they don't come home someone will look for them. They hope to be found in time to stop the robbery planned for the next morning.

### "Lucky Horseshoe"

Jim Burke (Tom Keene as Richard Powers) has plans to make himself a rich man, but not by using any legal paths.

He blackmails Poke Hanna (William Fawcett) into giving up his freight contract to carry supplies to the Indians but not before forcing him to give up half of the goods to Burke and only take half to the Indians for the rest of his tenure. Burke has plans to take over the freight route and skip the middle man.

He's selling the stolen goods at his store in Black Rock at cheap prices, which is sending Judge Wiley's general store in Wileyville into bankruptcy.

When Burke offers to buy out the Judge and Bill finds shady characters with Hanna, who says they were hired as bodyguards, Bill knows the whole mess needs investigating.

It's a twisted tale of blackmail, winning a freight contract and the importance of reporting threats to the law, as well as protecting the Indian welfare in order to keep the peace.

## "Pawnee Stampede"

"Pawnee Stampede" brings one of the land rushes used to open new land in the Old West to Wileyville.

Calamity gallops into town as if something is chasing her and almost bowls over Indian Agent Barry Copeland (Myron Healey) as she dashes for the store to tell the Judge that the land commissioner is on the incoming stage. She tells Copeland, too.

The people of Wileyville hope that the land commissioner will authorize a land run on the Pawnee Strip. The Reverend Jeff Palmer (Leonard Penn) has been one of the chief hopers because he wants land to build a church.

The Judge sends Bill and Calamity out to welcome the official. However, the commissioner is getting another kind of welcome from Copeland's henchmen, Stan (Rick Vallin) and Vic (Sandy Sanders), one filled with lead. Bill rides up in time to chase them away but not before the land commissioner is killed. The killers ride into the Pawnee Strip and Bill stops because he has no authority there. It's becoming a haven for outlaws because there is no law, which is one of the major reasons the Judge wants a land run.

The henchmen report to Copeland and arrive as he is telling Chief White Bird (John War Eagle) he will keep the white men off Indian land as long as the tribe continues to pay him.

In the commissioner's papers Bill finds permission to petition for the land run. Two thousand signatures will authorize it.

The Reverend joins them to print and post notices but Stan and Vic thwart their every effort and finally they are forced to see every citizen in person. However, they do it and the rush is set.

Copeland still has a scheme to turn things to his advantage. The challenge is for Bill to find out in time and stop it.

"Pawnee Stampede" contains one of the most annoying sequences in the series. The Reverend takes non-violence to the point of absurdity. When Calamity hits Stan on the head to keep him from shooting Bill in the back, Palmer tells her he doesn't approve of her actions. Oh! Please! This is the frontier. If screenwriters Robert Schaefer and Eric Freiwald couldn't figure that out, it seems like veteran director George Archainbaud would have. It's one of those "in a hurry to get it done" glitches.

## "Rails Westward"

Silas Greeley (Stanley Andrews) and his daughter Rowena (Fran Bennett) are on the stage to Wileyville when driver Jed Bascom (Dennis Moore) pulls up the team and looks into the distance through a spyglass. He sees telegraph lines being strung but tells the Greeleys he was watching some Indians.

Bill meets the stage and is infatuated by Rowena. He offers to help them any way he can as long as they are in Wileyville and he hopes they will settle there.

Bascom goes in to tell his boss, Larry Carter (Bill Henry), that telegraph lines are going through Wingate Pass, which means the railroad is coming to Wileyville.

Carter tells him to keep it quiet. He may sell the stage line before anyone else finds out the railroad is coming.

"Rails Westward" has two storylines. The other, which will entwine with the main plot before the story ends, involves Carter's unfair treatment of the Indians. The Judge fines him and the stage line owner says publicly he may sell out.

Greeley will consider investing in a business in Wileyville if the right opportunity presents itself. Carter tells Bill he'll pay a commission for help in finding a buyer for the line.

It all sounds good but Greeley turns on Bill when news of the railroad breaks and Bascom kills Carter and blames Bill's Indian friend. Bill has a lot to straighten out in this episode.

## "The Rain Wagon"

The drought is hard on the ranchers. Tempers are short. When Joseph Quigley (Lyle Talbot) at the express office refuses a loan to Jan Peterson (John Doucette), Peterson throttles him but Bill pulls him off. In the struggle Peterson drops his pipe.

Soon a rain wagon comes to town. In flowery language laced with Shakespearean misquotes Osgood Falstaff (Dick Elliot) introduces himself as the rainmaker and Bardolph Higgins (Lane Bradford) as his assistant. Falstaff promises a demonstration of his rainmaking prowess the next morning. He makes a deal with Judge Wiley to park his wagon in the barnyard overnight.

Calamity is fascinated and can't resist climbing on the wagon to look around. Higgins catches her and is about to hit her when Bill comes to her rescue. Higgins and Bill are fighting when Falstaff returns. He chastises Higgins and offers to make up for the trouble by letting Bill and Calamity sit on the wagon seat for the demonstration. Calamity is delighted. Bill declines.

The next morning when the street is filled with heavy, black smoke, Higgins slips into the express office. Bill hears shots fired at the office and runs there to find Quigley creased by a bullet and a story about a robbery and the pipe falling out of the robber's pocket. Quigley says the bandit was masked but he is sure it was Peterson who stole the $20,000, since the pipe has his initials.

Bill goes out to pick up Peterson and tells Calamity to keep an eye on the rainmakers. Still enamored, she thinks it's silly but succumbs to the lure of the wagon. Exploring it, she finds the express bag filled with money and barely has time to hide in the wagon before the rainmakers load up and leave town for their next stop.

When Bill gets back and learns Calamity is missing he goes after the rain wagon to find his sister and bring in the crooks.

### "Red Hawk"

Jess Sunday (Stanley Andrews) owns a freight line. He faithfully makes empty runs to the site of a worked out silver mine because he believes that new digging there will produce a rich strike.

A stagecoach pulls up behind him, making his team startle. Two of Ward Dawson's (Bill Henry) henchmen stop to make fun of him and spook his team, throwing him back into the wagon and knocking him out. Bill comes along in time to stop the runaway.

When they all come together in Wileyville, a confrontation takes place between Dawson, his henchmen, Sunday and Bill. Much expository dialog reveals the situation involving the mine and the conflict between Dawson and Sunday. Jess is running the regular empty silver runs so that the freight line will be profitable when silver is found. He's doing all this for his son Red Hawk (Michael Hall), who will soon be home from college in the East.

The rich silver strike is made. Now Dawson wants the freight contract, too, and will do anything to get it. Hugh Clemens (Kenne Duncan), who manages the mine, knows of Sunday's efforts and favors him but Dawson insists his claim be considered, too.

When Clemens learns that Sunday's son is an adopted Indian, he has doubts and Dawson is just the one to play on anti-Indian prejudice to try to steal the opportunity Jess has worked for so long by any means available.

Bill and the Judge must uphold the banner of fairness and help Red Hawk receive his rightful heritage.

### "Redskin Gap"

Butch Cassidy (Harry Lauter) makes an appearance in "Redskin Gap."

In this episode Wileyville is located not far from the Mexican border, for which Cassidy and the Wild Bunch are headed.

The character who mans the crossing is an old sailor, Barnacle Barney (Hank Patterson), whose longing for the sea has caused him to deck out the border station like the bridge of a ship. Calamity is fascinated and in "Redskin Gap" has abandoned the telegraph for learning to signal with semaphore flags.

The stage that arrives is carrying $100,000 in currency but the driver (Bob Woodward) has no concerns about leaving the stage because Marshal Jeffrey (Gregg Barton) stays with the coach.

He should have felt uneasy because Butch jumps into the driver's seat and steals the whole stage. The marshal climbs up and handcuffs Cassidy but a fight ensues and both fall from the stage.

When Bill stops the runaway and backtracks the road, he finds the real marshal knocked cold with Cassidy wearing the badge, carrying the marshal's ID and identifying the unconscious man as Butch Cassidy.

Butch convinces the Judge to hold "Cassidy" in the Wileyville jail while he, the "marshal," goes after the Wild Bunch.

Bill and Calamity are cleaning up the store when Bill finds a wanted poster for Cassidy with a picture of the man they have believed is the marshal on it. They head out to set things straight. Calamity's signaling lessons prove invaluable to their efforts.

With plenty of action and humorous ins and outs, "Redskin Gap" is one of the top episodes.

## "Roughshod"

Miguel Estrada (Victor Millan) is a fine artist but his father Tomas (Julian Rivero) considers it foolishness. Tomas has much to worry about. Walt Chantry (Harry Lauter) wants his land to add to the holdings of his boss, Cherokee Charlie Kerns (Harry Woods), a Chicago financier and art collector known as the "Empire Builder."

Chantry sends his henchman Sundown (Lane Bradford) with a gang to stampede the sheep, which almost trample Calamity before Bill rides in to rescue her.

Bill sends Calamity for Judge Wiley, who arrives in time to stop Tomas from going after Chantry with a gun.

Kerns only comes to the ranch once or twice a year and this is the time he usually visits. The Judge says he will talk to him.

Chantry and Sundown go to meet Cherokee's train. Chantry tells Sundown he wants no one talking to the boss but Sundown assures him the boss hasn't a clue to the amount being stolen from him on all the land transactions Chantry has been making.

When Kerns arrives, he pays the stage driver and takes over the stagecoach. Then he tells Bill he won't talk to the Judge. He's used to having his own way. But Bill chases the stage, jumps onto it and takes Cherokee to the Judge at gunpoint.

After a session with Kerns, the Judge sends Bill out to talk to all the ranchers that Chantry has bought out. They need to prove to Cherokee that his manager has been cheating not only the ranchers but also his boss and convince Cherokee that his manager is the villain of the story.

## "Runaway Renegade"

"Runaway Renegade" begins with the Judge in his nightclothes raging when he arises to find the store has been robbed. Bill goes after the thief and finds that the culprit is a young boy, Bobby (Sammy Ogg), who refuses to give them his last name.

Kelso Dodge (James Griffith) and Frank Patterson (Lane Bradford) ride into Wileyville and come into the store seeking information about a man they are hunting for murder, Tom Bishop (Walter Reed). Bobby bursts from the living quarters behind the store to defend him.

After a nicely done fight between Bill and Patterson and the exit of the pursuers, Bill and the Judge convince Bobby to let them help his father, who has never been given a chance to tell his side of the story.

With help from Bill, Bishop is able to prove his innocence and Dodge and Patterson, the real killers, are captured.

### "Secret of the Silverado"

Silver is being smuggled across the border near Wileyville.

Bill and his friend Tony Castelar (Neyle Morrow) have a plan to capture the smuggling ring. Tony will go undercover and try to get in with the gang by pretending to smuggle silver from his own source in hopes the real crooks seek him out.

Bill "catches" Tony driving a wagon of Mexican silver across the border. When Judge Wiley holds court, he brags about the amount of silver he still has but won't tell the Judge anything else. The Judge throws him in jail, hoping that the smuggling ring will break him out to find the source of his silver.

Sure enough, it works. A stranger slips a gun and a note through the bars and when he escapes takes him to Hank Dawson (Keith Richards), who offers Tony a deal if he will throw in with them and bring his silver to be smuggled with theirs. Tony asks how can they do it any easier than he can alone, to which Dawson replies, "organization." Tony agrees but insists that he bring his silver rather than tell them where his is.

Bill and Tony are using Calamity, masquerading as a Mexican taco seller, to pass messages back and forth. She tells Bill that Lafe Collins (Mike Ragan), owner of the Silverado mine, is involved. Bill goes out to take a look.

He discovers that the Silverado mine and El Cortez mine in Mexico are linked, making a perfect underground passageway to smuggle silver. Bill and Tony meet in the middle.

As usual, Calamity had followed Bill and before he explored in the mine he had sent her back for the Judge for help.

Good thing, because Tony and Bill are caught in the mines and can use a little help to wrap up the crooks.

## "Silver Mine Mystery"

Silver shipments have been running short. Driver Ben Goodman (Edgar Dearing) starts his wagon on his run into Wileyville with a load and the intention of talking to Judge Wiley about the situation.

Drew Felton (Stacey Harris) and his henchmen, Farrel (Dennis Moore) and Retlow (Kirk Alyn), have doctored the wagon to blow up and kill Goodman before he can talk.

The wagon blows but Goodman survives. He is found by Bill and Calamity, on their way to the mine with a delivery, who take him to a near-by hunter's shack to patch him up.

Bill suggests that if whoever tried to kill Goodman believes him dead, another attempt on his life won't be made.

Judge Wiley and the mine owner, Tom Caraway (Gayne Whitman) discover the wreckage on their way to the mine. When they get to the mine they hold a hearing and, because Goodman's body is missing, the Judge determines he stole the silver and ran away. He also impounds all the mine records and has Bill stay at the mine overnight to bring them to Wileyville in the morning. This is not good news for the baddies. They must prevent those records from being examined.

Bill is sure Felton, not Goodman, is the thief and sets out to prove it by masquerading as Goodman's ghost. The henchmen who fight with him are sure he had too much punch for a ghost but they don't know he found the solution to what has been happening to the missing silver.

Now if he can only stay alive long enough to tell the mine owner and the Judge.

## "Six-Gun Symphony"

"Six-Gun Symphony" is almost a lost episode. On most DVDs that profess to sell it, "Runaway Renegade" is the entry that is shown. Internet Movie Database goes right along with the blunder, showing the cast and characters from "Runaway Renegade" as the cast of "Six-Gun Symphony" instead of the performers who are actually in it.

"Runaway Renegade" has been previously discussed. The cast includes Walter Reed, Sammy Ogg, James Griffith and Lane Bradford. It is about baddies chasing a man to blame the crime they committed on him.

The "Six-Gun Symphony" cast includes John Doucette, Lyle Talbot, Lane Bradford (once again) and Dick Shackleton. This plot involves a noisy roadhouse on the outskirts of Wileyville and a professional gambler and his son.

"Six-Gun Symphony" is filled with humor and no killings – just fights. It's kind of *Buffalo Bill, Jr. Lite.*

Danny Foster (Dick Shackleton) comes into the store to buy ammunition. Calamity gets out a box of shells, then hesitates. She doubts that Judge Wiley would approve of her selling them to someone Danny's age.

Danny grabs the box when Calamity goes to ask Bill about the sale, so Bill goes after him. He chases Danny to Larson's road-house just outside of Wileyville.

Outside of the establishment, Mrs. Henley (Loie Bridge) and Mrs. Milburne (Kathryn Sheldon) sit in a buckboard waiting for Hank Willis (Hal K. Dawson) to come out. They are members of the auxiliary of the Law and Order League and he has broken his promise not to gamble at the roadhouse. They ask Bill, whom they call William, to send him out. They are the one of the recurring comic elements of this episode.

Bill goes in, snatches the box of shells from Danny, and tells Hank the ladies are waiting for him. Danny punches Bill then Tex Greer (Lane Bradford) jumps in. It's a good fight, one of many scenes in the episode choreographed to show off Bill's physical prowess.

When the fight starts, Jim Larson (John Doucette) gives Hank a nickel to put in the music box because the ladies don't like to hear fighting.

Larson goes out to the ladies and spooks their horses. He blocks Bill's path one way and Tex the other and Bill is forced to jump over three horses to get to his own and race to stop the runaway.

The ladies go straight to the Judge and demand that he close Larson's roadhouse. The Judge points out that he has no jurisdiction because the place is a half-mile from the town limits.

Then the music box cranks up again and that does it. The Judge makes an ordinance extending the town limits for five miles in all directions and they all troop out to watch him shut down the gambling house.

Larson and Tex see them coming and tell everyone inside to hide all the traces of gambling. Larson tells Ace Foster (Lyle Talbot), Danny's father, to put the money in the vault. He does, but then has an idea and quickly takes it out again and hides it.

During another good fight sequence, he staggers from the office saying two masked men stole the money.

Every time a fight starts, Larson has someone put a nickel in the music box, another recurring comic scene. Calamity also has a comic motif. She has a broom or mop in her hand that she tries to use as a weapon, inevitably hitting Bill.

When the dust settles, the Judge takes them all to court in Wileyville. He fines Larson and Tex for running a gambling house; he sends Danny to school.

Bill comes in saying he has looked all over and can find no tracks of the two horses of the men who robbed the roadhouse. He suggests that Foster was in with somebody and the descriptions he gave were phony. With that in mind, the Judge gives Ace thirty days for letting Danny hang around the gambling den and says maybe in that time he will also remember what happened to the money.

Bill figures out that maybe Foster took the money for himself but he must do his shift guarding the prisoner because the cell lock is broken.

He sends Calamity out to search the office of the roadhouse and gives her a nickel for protection. She can put it in the music box if she needs help.

Danny, Larson and Tex break Ace out of jail. When Larson asks about the money, Foster tells him he gave it to a friend to hide and the friend rode to Flagstaff. He suggests they split up for the trip. He and Danny will meet Larson and Tex in Flagstaff.

"Flagstaff" proves to be only half a mile from the Wileyville store. At the roadhouse.

Calamity will have to use the nickel Bill gave her.

## "Tough Tenderfoot"

Three masked men break into the law office of Judge Wiley's friend, Tom Jenkins (Charlie Hayes), shoot him and begin ransacking the place looking for the will of Ian MacDazey.

Judge Wiley has sent Bill and Calamity to borrow a book from Jenkins. Bill walks in on the men and fights them but they get away.

Going home, the two hear a strange noise and stop to investigate. They meet the Laird of Killkraile (Leo Britt) from Scotland, who travels with a servant, Pancho (Nacho Galindo), a phonograph to play bagpipe music and a caber to throw.

The three baddies also ride up, but Alex MacDazey (Fred Colby) knows exactly who the Laird is. He is the cousin from Scotland to whom Ian MacDazey left his mine with the newly discovered gold strike. Alex intends to see that his cousin never gets it.

When the Laird goes to the MacDazey shack to meet his cousin, he gets a rough welcome. Pancho faints from the stress.

Bill and Calamity, out riding again, arrive in time for Bill to chase the wagon into which the bound up Laird has been thrown before the horses were spooked. Bill stops the runaway but, in the confusion, the unconscious Pancho is left behind.

Pancho comes to and makes a noise. Alex and his henchmen capture him and plan to kill him.

At Wileyville, the Judge and Bill are making the Laird welcome and discussing what can be done about MacDazey. To make a point, the Judge opens one of the books his friend Jenkins willed him and Ian MacDazey's will falls out. Its contents make it obvious what Alex has been up to and the three head out to find Pancho and bring the villains to justice.

When asked about this episode Dick replied:

*I watched the episode where the guy was from Scotland and tossing the caber. I don't know who the actor who played the Scotsman is, never worked with him before and don't remember his name. I never saw him in anything afterward.*

## "Trail of the Killer"

Billy the Kid (Chuck Courtney) and Charlie Bowdre (Henry Rowland) pay a visit to Wileyville in "Trail of the Killer."

When The Kid first rides in, Calamity just knows he's Billy the Kid but Bill is skeptical. Just as Calamity has Bill convinced, Bowdre rides in wearing the badge of the sheriff they killed and tells them The Kid is one of his deputies. Calamity apologizes but still has doubts and before the story ends, Calamity's suspicions prove to be true.

Pat Garrett comes through town and Bill is able to help in the capture The Kid. The final narration of the episode has the Judge reading the rest of the Billy the Kid legend from the newspaper.

Tidbits in this episode are the well-choreographed fight between Dick Jones and Chuck Courtney, both experienced stunt fighters; for horse lovers, the gorgeous dapple gray that Courtney rides; and the fact that Jimmie Dodd, famous to kids of that era as the MC on the original Mickey Mouse Club, has an uncredited line reading about Billy the Kid's escapades from a posted notice. The screenplay was by Maurice Geraghty, who wrote B-Westerns in the thirties.

Dick remembered the horse.

*In "Trail of the Killer," Chuck Courtney, who played Billy the Kid, rode a dapple gray horse. George Sponx supplied that horse and Cisco Kid's horse. That dapple gray was in* The Strawberry Roan. *The girl rode the dapple gray. That dapple gray was used in a lot of pictures, a real good horse.*

## "Trouble Thompson"

The title character in the "Trouble Thompson" episode is a clown in a traveling show. He stays in a jam so often that he believes he personifies his name.

When the show wagon with Trouble (Syd Saylor) and show owner Sinclair (Joseph Greene) is robbed, Sinclair fires Trouble in exasperation, even though Bill came along in time to get most of the money back.

Calamity is thrilled to meet "the clown on the poster" and takes him home with them, promising that Judge Wiley will have a job he can do. The Judge isn't pleased but agrees to take in Trouble.

The show has reached Wileyville and all of its cash is in the Wileyville bank, which just happens to have caught the eye of the robbers and is their next target. They escape with all the money but one of the outlaws is wounded.

Sinclair once again blames Trouble for the bank robbery and Trouble's self-esteem is so low that he starts packing to leave Wileyville. The Judge and Bill insist that he should stay and try to cheer up Calamity – through the window, as the Judge, with his doctor hat on, has just quarantined her with the measles.

Meanwhile, the outlaw leader (Stacey Harris) has devised a plan to sucker the Judge out onto the road so they can capture him to doctor the wounded gang member. The Judge manages to send his mule, Old Nelly, back home to get help. Trouble refuses to hear "no" and goes with Bill to rescue the Judge.

# Stories from the Road

Making public appearances was a part of the Flying A contract. Dick and Jock Mahoney logged many a mile on the road promoting *The Range Rider* when they were not filming.

Stories from the road were some of Dick's favorites to tell when he talked about *The Range Rider years*. He told them willingly and as often as they were requested. These versions are the ones he recorded for inclusion in a book of his memoirs. They are in his words, the first of which were, "The Range Rider? I know too much about him."

*I have lots of road show memories. I remember one time when the McCarthy investigation was going on in Washington, D.C., we had a show in Washington, D.C., at the same time and there were more cowboys in the arena than there were people in the audience. When we closed the show, the manager brought the money and it was divided up – so much for the cowboys, so much for the rodeo stock, so much for Jock and so much for me. My share was fifty cents.*

*Cowboys got paid first, the stock contractor got second and what was left over Jock and I split.*

*That one was real bad but we went to Philadelphia right after that and we really cleaned up. Full houses. Twenty-some-odd performances.*

The road trips were not injury-free and the injuries often stood out in Dick's mind as he reminisced.

*The very first one we did was like a rodeo but it was a circus in Pittsburg. I remember we watched this miniscule lady do a high trapeze act with no net. Jocko and I sat there on our horses and said, "Boy! She's crazy."*

*Then when we came charging down the third base line and got shot off our horses and fell on the track and they thought we were crazy. When we started the fight and tore up all the furniture and busted everything up around there, they knew we were crazy.*

*I sprained my ankle or something because I had to use epichloride to freeze my ankle so I could get my boot off and use it again to put my boot on. I messed it up pretty bad. I didn't come home with the horses that time. They left before we were through so we flew from Pittsburg home. I remember Jock and I were sitting up – spread out – in first class and I was using Absorbine – not Absorbine, Jr., but what they use on horses – on my ankle. The stewardess came by and said, "You guys have got to stop using that. You're getting all my passengers sick." It's strong but it was the only way I could hang on to it.*

*I have lots of tales to tell about the rodeo shows.*

*The first one we did was the Houston stock show. I forget which year it was we were down there. That was a fun show because they're big party people down there and they wouldn't leave us alone to get any rest. They always wanted to party.*

*I did a fight scene in that thing. We'd set up a living room and Jocko would launch himself over a couch and two big overstuffed chairs and a big dining room table – you could jump up and down on it – and a kitchen-type chair that we could beat each other over the head with.*

*One part of it, he'd come diving over the table and I'm supposed to catch him and guide him over the couch so he doesn't kill himself and he came down on my hand – I got my hand in the wrong position – and dislocated all four fingers.*

*So the next night when he comes at me and I'm supposed to grab him, my fingers were bent back and I just swung by him.*

*I said, "Hey, look. Dislocated."*

*So he turns around and says, "Hold the phone," and he reaches over and grabs my hand and goes cra-aack and puts them back in place and we go on with the show.*

*It took a long time to get my fingers back so they would work all right but we went on with the show. Somebody said, "The show must go on."*

*Another time Jocko said that to me and I wanted to kill him. I can't remember where it was. Cleveland, maybe. I got blood poisoning and I puffed up like a balloon. They gave me sulfa and I'm allergic to sulfa. My eyes were closed. I couldn't bend my fingers.*

*I remember him putting me up on my horse and the overture was playing. The band was blowing up a storm.*

*He said, "Come on. We gotta go."*

*I said, "Uh-uh."*

*He said, "The show must go on."*

*I said, "I'll kill him."*

*Then they opened the gate and we went out and did the show.*

*Another one was in Cincinnati. You know, in indoor arenas they change it from ice rink one night to rodeo arena with tanbark on it. After we finished in the arena we'd do our bows and run the horses backward out of the arena – the horses ran as fast backward as frontward – waving our hats. My horse went through the tanbark and hit the terrazzo and slid and his feet went right under him. He went over backward so fast I couldn't get out of the saddle. I got caught and he landed on top of me. The saddle horn got me in the pelvis area and I knew I was hurt, so I grabbed the saddle horn so that when he went to get up I would be with him.*

*There was so much strain that he broke the front cinch and slid back to the back cinch and that's the same thing you put on a horse to make him buck. He started bucking and Bang! He hit me with both barrels, both hind legs. One of them got me in the jaw and the horseshoe mark on my shoulder must have been the first one because*

*Some of the action fans saw during fight demonstrations on the road.*

*if he'd hit me in the head with that force in the face, it would have torn my head off. But all it did was just cut my lip and my tongue and turned me a flip and I landed face down in the arena.*

*I'm lying down there in the arena and look up at the audience – there's still a blackout – and I see this white figure up in the audience flying down like a dove and I recognized it's Betty [Dick's wife]. She's got on a white stole. I hear her running down, screaming and I think, "What the hell does she think she's gonna do?"*

*I'm face down in the mud and the blood and the goo and Jock comes out and picks me up and says, "If you can't ride out, I'll walk out with you." And we walk out waving our hats. I passed out in the dressing room. I come to and Betty's got a burlap gunny sack and she's wiping the dirt off my face and that scratched like hell. She wasn't doing any good at trying to help me.*

*They stuck me in the hospital and put me in traction because I fractured my pelvis bone and they went to a party. That was the last show of the day. I said, "I can't stand this," so I got my pants and got my pocket knife out and cut all the strings and ropes they had me tied up with in this traction stuff and I got a cab and went to the party.*

Some of the injury stories took an amusing twist, such as Jock's injury in Boston. Dick told this story many times and a version of it appears in Gene Freese's biography of Jock, *Jock Mahoney: The Life and Films of a Hollywood Stuntman*.

Here is the way Dick recorded it for his memoirs:

*We were headliners in Boston. The first time we were co-stars with Gene Autry. The second time we were headliners.*

*About the fourth or fifth show, Jocko hit the tanbark when he did a saddlefall and he didn't slide. It was like he stuck his head in the bucket and cracked his body – didn't even double – and pulled all the tendons in his ribcage. He was really hurting.*

*In the hotel, he was moaning and groaning and stretching and trying to get comfortable. He was flat out in the middle of the floor and all he had was a towel. He was wrapping it around his neck trying to put some pressure to straighten his neck out.*

*I said, "I'm sick and tired of all your moaning and groaning. I'm just going down to get something to read."*

*He said, "Well, while you're down there bring up some dancing girls and we'll have a party."*

*I said, "Okay. Dancing girls."*

*So I go down into the lobby and when I get out of the elevator door here are all these — must've been a dozen of them — seventeen- or eighteen-year-old girls all in white formals. Daughters at a party or something like that.*

*I walked out of the elevator and they started, "Oh, Dickie West! Dickie West! Where's the Range Rider?"*

*I said, "The Range Rider? You want to see the Range Rider?"*

*"Oh, yes, yes, yes, yes."*

*I said, "Come on." So I loaded that elevator up with these beautiful young ladies and up we go. We go from the elevator to our suite, big double doors. I swung the doors open and ushered them in and said, "Ladies, the Range Rider."*

*There he is, lying on the floor with nothing but a towel.*

*He looks up and says, "Oh, you son-of-a-bitch."*

*I left him with all those girls and I don't know what the outcome was. All those girls and nothing but a towel. The little girls didn't run out screaming and hollering. I didn't stick around to see. I figured he'd be after me and want to kill me, so I was gone.*

The rodeo appearances always started with the Range Rider and Dick West on horseback.

*We were out in the middle of the arena, then afterwards we could be close up with the fans. I enjoyed that, particularly indoor shows because they could black everything out and put the spot on us.*

*I would listen for some little kid to giggle and when I'd hear that I'd start acting toward that. One of the gags was that if one little girl was giggling real hard, I'd run at it and jump the wall and Jock would have to chase after me and drag me back in. That would get a big laugh from the little kids. It was fun.*

*Jocko giving invocation, Dick with head bowed.*

*Arena publicity pose.*

That fit with the Dick West persona and his infatuation with every girl he met on *The Range Rider* shows.

All of the road stories did not involve injury but often spun around adventures traveling with Jocko.

*When we were doing the shows and providing the stock, handling our stunt equipment, I would go in with our truck and our horses and get that stuff set up. Jock would go in earlier and do most of the yakking with the dignitaries and go to the hospitals and stuff like that. If we had time, then I would go. I didn't get caught on it all the time.*

*Jock had no sense of the importance of money.*

*Another time, the first trip to Houston, Fred Krone and I were loading up after the final show, getting all the stuff together and I'm packing up.*

*Jock comes up and said, "You got any more room to take this home so I don't hafta take it on the airplane?" It looked like a package of laundry – the way they do shirts up and stack them and wrap them in a bundle. It looked like a bundle of shirts.*

*I said, "Yeah, I got room if you let me open them up and spread them out."*

*He said, "Sure. Go ahead."*

*So he's out the door and when I get around to opening the thing up there's $10,000 in one-dollar bills in that package. That's all they could come up with because we demanded cash and they gave him cash for the last day.*

*So here I am with $10,000. It's Sunday. There're no banks open and I'm going to be carrying this all the way back to California. We had that mostly in a horse stall in the trailer and in the gear for the horses and footlockers.*

*He thought that was funny. And Fred and I worried about that money, traveling all the way back to California.*

A personal favorite of the Jock-on-the-road stories that Dick told often, we titled, "Jock and the Roses."

*We'd been on the road about ninety days and done about seven shows starting off with Rhode Island – little shows, not Madison Square Garden or Boston Garden. We had the stock and we put on the show.*

*We were in Cleveland and we'd been gone a long time and we were going to wrap it up and Jock said, "Why don't we get the girls to come on out here and spend the last couple of days with us and we'll party it up? And then you go up and pick up your new car in Rhode Island and Maggie and I will do something."*

*"Boy! Will I be glad to see her! You know what I'm going to do?"*

*I said, "I haven't the foggiest."*

*He said, "I'm going to buy every rose they have in town and I'm going to fill the hotel suite up with roses, red roses. I'm going to greet her at the door with nothing on but a rose in my teeth and say, 'Maggie!' "*

*I said, "You don't want to do that."*

*He said, "Why not?"*

*I said, "There's gonna be a bellboy and he's going to open the door and usher her in. You'll scare him half to death."*

*"Oh, yeah, I forgot about that. Okay, I'll hide in the shower."*

*I was going to say, "Don't do that," because the bellboy goes in. He looks in the closets, he pulls the curtain back in the shower. Then I thought, no I'll let him find out for himself.*

*So the next day I see him and I said, "Well, how did it go? How did Maggie like all the roses?"*

*He said, "You son-of-a-bitch. You didn't tell me the bellboy was gonna look in the shower."*

*I asked, "What'd you do?"*

*He said, "I said, 'Hello.' "*

Another often-told tale concerned problems resulting from dealings with television production staff when they did the *Ed Sullivan Show.*

*Jocko's the one that knew how to make a fight scene look real – how to throw a punch and make it look like it tore a head off.*

*To give an example of the way you make it look good: We did a fight on . . . the guy [Ed Sullivan] that always had some celebrity on his show in New York . . . I'll think of it. Anyway we did a fight scene. That's a whole story in itself the way they'd say, "Uh-huh. Uh-huh."*

*And Jocko'd say, "We need this tied down and we need this anchored down or it'll get messed up."*

*And they kept saying, "Uh-huh. Uh-huh. And we'll give you four stuntmen to work with."*

*They had them sitting at a table playing cards and we get up on the balcony and we're looking down at where we're going to fall when it came time to do it. We went through the rail and look down and those four took off whining.*

*Jock said, "You take the left, I'll take the right," and we crashed into the table. When they scattered, they turned the table upside down. We were going to use it to break our fall and all we're looking at is four legs of the table. We kind of got around them and kept on going.*

*The last big mess was when he knocked me over the bar into the back bar and that's when we absolutely, completely destroyed the set they were going to use the next day with Elvis Presley.*

*We told them that thing won't just stand there. But they said, "Oh, yeah. Oh, yeah."*

*When we got back to Madison Square Garden Jocko said, "You watched it. What did you think of it?" They [the wives] said, "Everything was fine until that last punch, it looked like you missed him."*

*I said, "Oh, yeah," and turned around and showed them the biggest shiner you ever saw in your life. He actually hit me and it didn't sell. It looked like a miss.*

Personal appearances were also made for groups of children who might not otherwise get to see their heroes. Dick and Jocko were not strangers to the hospitals and kids' organizations on their path.

*We made all the hospitals, particularly the pediatric wards where the little kids were. That's tough work.*

*Dick (on floor playing horsey) and Jock (kneeling) visit with young fans on a personal appearance tour.*

*We were in one where they had a bunch of little bitty kids – four-or five-years old or so. I must've had ten of them hanging onto me, one on each finger. They just hang on like there's no tomorrow. That really tore me up but that was part of what we did.*

Meeting Dick Jones was always a thrill for his fans. One of the special opportunities for devotees of *The Range Rider* show came at the Memphis Film Festival in 1987. It was the only time the Range Rider and Dick West appeared together at a Western festival after the personal appearance tours of the 1950s.

Dick arrived the evening before Jocko and remembers when they came face-to-face at the event the next day.

*At the Memphis Film Festival one year, Jock came in the day after I did and was sitting at the table signing autographs.*

*One of his pet peeves was that somebody would give you a scrap of paper and want your autograph. He'd say. "Please. You get a better autograph with a better piece of paper." That really bugged him.*

*So I got in line and hid out as the line moved all the way up there. The smallest piece of paper I could get was a gum wrapper. I opened it up and got right up to him. He had his head down with his hat over his eyes so he couldn't see. He was autographing like crazy.*

*I shoved this wrapper right under his nose and said, "Give me your autograph."*

*He did a slow burn when he looked at that piece of paper and looked up and said, "Oh, you son-of-a-bitch!" That's the only time we worked a film festival together. It was a long time after the rodeos.*

*Jock's slow burn.*          *"Oh, you . . ."*          *Enjoying the joke.*

In his later years, after retirement, Dick was a welcome guest at a number of film festivals. He was kindness itself to his fans [as was Jocko before his death in 1989]. Dick especially loved to meet and have pictures made with youngsters.

One of his pet peeves was charging for autographs, which is now the standard at these conventions. When pressure from other celebrity guests became intense, he put a jar on his table. All the money he took in from autographs went to charity.

# Remembering
# Dick Jones

As a child, I loved *Buffalo Bill, Jr.* It came on in my hometown at 10:30 on Saturday mornings and I never missed it. I wanted Bill for my big brother and was so jealous of Calamity. (When I met Nancy Gilbert, I told her that. She laughed.)

I was too young for *The Range Rider* and it was not until I was an adult that I saw those wonderful, action-packed shows.

It was a tremendous thrill to meet Dick Jones at the 1987 Memphis Film Festival when he and Jock Mahoney appeared together. (I had met Jocko previously.) It was my pleasure to be able to go to the airport to greet them upon arrival. Talk about excited!

One of my most treasured photographs is of me standing between the two of them at the banquet of that festival.

During that event, Dick and I shared conversation, meals and card games, watched movies together and began a friendship that lasted until his death on July 7, 2014.

Over the years, we got together at festivals, had phone conversations and exchanged correspondence, although he billed himself "The World's Worst Correspondent." I never challenged his claim.

His wife Betty, a lovely lady and delightful company, came to festivals with him. We exchanged Christmas cards and notes, vis-

*The author with the Range Rider and Dick West at the 1987 Memphis Film Festival.*

ited over the miles via phone and developed a warm relationship.

Always a lover of Westerns, I wrote my first book on Western movies years ago. Dick wrote the forward for my book. He and Betty were a part of my life.

Some fifteen years ago, when I was working on a book on stuntman Cliff Lyons, Betty suggested that I should write up Dick's stories of his years in films and on television. I was willing. Dick was not.

For years, Betty and I cajoled and tried every tack to persuade Dick to let me record his memories. Again and again he refused.

Finally in 2010, Dick relented. We started a series of phone interviews, which I taped and transcribed. He was adamant that only what he wanted included was recorded. When certain topics, including his family and personal life, were approached, he said, "I'm not going there," and that was the end of that path.

Anyone who knew Dick Jones knows exactly how that was with him. Dick was a very private person and just agreeing to talk for posterity at all was making quite a concession.

Two years later, I flew to California and spent several days scanning Dick's still collection into my computer, sleeping in their den with my computer on one TV tray, the scanner on another and working from daylight until late night. During much of the day, Betty sat and visited with me while I worked. It is a treasured time in my heart. As a result of Dick's generosity, I probably have a better collection of Dick Jones stills, lobby cards and other memorabilia than anyone other than the Jones family. Much of it is signed.

Then we hit a series of hang ups and delays. Speed had picked up again at the time of Dick's sudden death. I did not handle that well.

In time, I realized I needed to revisit the plan for the book. It will be presented in two parts. This book, *Dick Jones: Where the Action Was*, contains the stories from Dick's television series, *The Range Rider* and *Buffalo Bill, Jr.* He appeared in other television shows, which are identified, but his focus was on the series in which he starred. So is this account.

This book was not created because I heard about Dick Jones and thought he would be a good subject. (He was.) It is a tribute to a friend, whom I knew long before my first book was ever published.

It was spurred on by the drive of Dick's wife Betty, whose enthusiasm was contagious, and continued because the more I learned about the film work of Dickie Jones the more impressed I became. The more I watched and analyzed the amazing stunt work he and Jock Mahoney did, the more it blew me away.

Of all the work Dick did on screen, he was proudest of the stunt/action sequences he created and performed, so I have tried to emphasize action. That's what it was about for him and, in all honesty, the thing that I love and respect, too. Not pulling this all together was not an option.

A second volume is planned, focusing on Dick's early film career as a child actor, a handful of his later films and the experience of knowing Dick Jones.

When Dick died he had left instructions for no memorials, something that can be hard for those left behind. This is my memorial for Dick that I hope he would find acceptable, as he was a party to its creation.

# Annotated Sources

The most important sources for this book were the interviews with Dick Jones that I recorded over the years and the videos of the episodes of *The Range Rider* and *Buffalo Bill, Jr.* I say videos because the first ones I owned were in Beta format. Though a few were missing, most of the DVDs that replaced the tapes were obtained from Martin Grams, Jr. at a film festival. Searching through a variety of sellers, I managed to find all forty-two *Buffalo Bill, Jrs.* and seventy-seven of the seventy-eight *Range Riders*. This book would have been impossible without the ability to watch and re-watch these shows.

For supplemental information on the stuntmen, Neil Summers' column, "The Stuntmen," on the *Western Clippings* Web site (http://www.westernclippings.com) was extremely helpful. Also at that Web address is Boyd Magers' column on "Comic Book Cowboys," from which details about *The Range Rider* and *Buffalo Bill, Jr.* comic books were gathered. *Western Clippings* is also available in hard copy at 1312 Stagecoach Rd. SE, Albuquerque, NM 87123.

Another Web site I sometimes used for reference is The Old Corral (b-westerns.com). It has hard-to-find old pictures of hard-to-find old cowboys, a delight for fans of the genre.

Undated conversations over the years with some of the supporting players in the Flying A shows, as well as fans, were also helpful.

More than one visit to the Gene Autry Oklahoma Museum was made. The Dick Jones display is a must for his fans, but the building is chockfull of memorabilia of many cowboy heroes from both film and television. The museum has a web address for more information: https://www.geneautryokmuseum.com. The phone number there is 580-294-3047. It is open Wednesday though Saturday from 10 a.m. to 4 p.m.

Several books were valuable in gathering background information about the stock company players.

Brothers Tom and Jim Goldrup spent years compiling an impressive collection of interviews with supporting players, both in film and television, in four volumes. *Feature Players: The Stories Behind the Faces, Volumes 1–4* were privately printed.

It was a massive undertaking and an invaluable source for fans of old film. These interviews have been reformatted into a three-volume set, *The Encyclopedia of Feature Players of Hollywood*, Bear-Manor Media, 2012. They have a wealth of first-hand information about a herd of familiar faces to Western fans.

In 2005, Empire Publishing, Inc., Madison, North Carolina, published *Best of the Badmen (Polecats, Varmints, and Desperadoes of Western Films)* by three devoted fans and scholars of cowboy film history, Boyd Magers, Bob Nareau and Bobby Copeland. This fine reference book on the scoundrels who plagued the men in white hats includes a number of people who were on the Flying A team.

Another reference book on the Western stalwarts is the classic, *Western Films: Heroes, Heavies and Sagebrush* by Arthur F. McClure and Ken D. Jones, published in 1972 by A.S. Barnes and Company, South Brunswick and New York. This reliable resource has short sketches on a number of the stalwarts and baddies.

Gene Freese's book, *Jock Mahoney: The Life and Films of a Hollywood Stuntman*, was published in 2014 by McFarland & Company, Inc., Jefferson, North Carolina, and London. Dick read the chapter on *The Range Rider* and told me shortly before he died that it's all true, something he rarely said about information written about the series.

Many more sources exist for information about people mentioned in this book, but the body of research involved watching, re-watching and re-watching and watching still one more time the episodes of the two series, and listening to Dick's words about making them.

# Appendix I

## Other Television Appearances of Dick Jones

Dick was a guest on several television shows, most in the 1950s. The majority were on other Flying A series. Four appearances were on *Annie Oakley* and ten on *The Gene Autry Show*. He was on two other Western series, *The Lone Ranger* and *Wagon Train*, and the Civil War era series, *The Gray Ghost*. On the rest of the shows his character was involved with the military.

The role that stands out as different was as Billy Joe in a 1962 pilot for a show that did not sell, *The Night Rider*. The star was Johnny Cash and the plot was based on the Cash song, "Don't Take Your Guns to Town." It was a cast filled with singers. Merle Travis, Johnny Western, Eddie Dean and Gordon Terry sang around the campfire. Dick was the young man who took his guns to town, despite his mother's plea, and was killed by Johnny Cash in a gunfight.

Had this thirty-minute show sold, it might have been a hit, but not for Dick, since he was shot down in the pilot. DVDs of this show are available from several sources.

Dick's television appearances are listed below by series title. Episode titles are followed by the year they ran and the character Dick played, if known.

*The Lone Ranger*
    "Rustler's Hideout" (1949) Jim Patrick
    "Man Without a Gun" (1950) Jim Douglas
*The Gene Autry Show*
    "Gun Powder Range" (1950) Tim Parker
    "The Sheriff of Santa Rosa" (1950) Ted Doyle
    "Warning! Danger!" (1951) Jerry Miller
    "The Bandits of Boulder Bluff" (1951) Tom Colby
    "Horse Sense" (1952) Jeff Castle
    "The Western Way" (1952) Billy Walker

"The Sheriff Is a Lady" (1952) Horace, the Deputy Sheriff
"Santa Fe Raiders" (1954) Tim Morgan
"The Sharpshooter" (1954) Randy Barker
"Outlaw of Blue Mesa" (1954) Tom Jackson
*Mr. & Mrs. North*
   "Salt in His Blood" (1953) Chuck Walker
*Annie Oakley*
   "Annie and the Six o' Spades" (1954) Steve Donavan
   "Annie Helps a Drifter" (1954) Bob Neil
   "Annie Joins the Cavalry" (1954) Trooper Davis
   "Annie and the Junior Pioneers" (1955) Clell Morgan
*Navy Log*
   "The Leave" (1955)
*The Gray Ghost*
   "Renegade Rangers" (1957) Underwood
   "The Brothers" (1957) Ned
*Flight*
   "Bombs in the Belfry" (1958 or 1959)
*The Blue Angels*
   "Fire Flight" (1960) Bliss
*Wagon Train*
   "The Wagon Train Mutiny" (1962) John Hunter
*The Night Rider* (1962) Billy Joe

# Appendix II

## Episode Trivia

Most of the episode quirks are included with the commentary on individual episodes but a few extra comments could be made.

Many of the *Buffalo Bill, Jr.* episodes end with Bill and Calamity, and sometimes Judge Wiley, laughing together. That was standard for many programs made for children in that era.

A carryover from the days of the B-Western heroes who tried to be good moral examples for the youngsters who adored them was the occasional scene that encouraged prayer or preached a short moral lesson. In "The Silver Blade," the Range Rider comments that more prayer and faith would be good for everyone. In "Hooded Vengeance," Buffalo Bill, Jr. preaches the importance of doing what is right rather than being intimidated by threats. This principle is also promoted in the *Buffalo Bill, Jr.* episode, "The Lucky Horseshoe."

Settings were used and reused. Sometimes details appear to be an overlooked item that would have been better cleaned up. In "Romeo Goes West," when the Range Rider and Dick use Pettigew's wagon to enter the ghost town, the sign for Maw Manning's place that is a key location in "Trail of the Lawless" is prominently shown. The two episodes are not a pair, so it may be presumed that either these were made consecutive weeks or Maw Manning was a character in a film and the shot is stock footage.

One skill Jock Mahoney displayed in several episodes of *The Range Rider* was swordplay. Played as a part of fight scenes or for a bit of humor, these sequences are sure smile-bringers.

Some episodes of *Buffalo Bill, Jr.* and *The Range Rider* are readily available from a variety of sources. All are public domain, though certain companies copyright their individual production format. Other episodes are rare and only found through specialty sources.

Among the easily obtained, highly watchable *Buffalo Bill, Jr.*

episodes are "Fight for Geronimo," "First Posse," "The Death of Johnny Ringo," "Redskin Gap" and "Runaway Renegade." All of these have excellent displays of Dick's riding and stunting abilities and are nicely scripted.

Good episodes of The Range Rider located without difficulty include "Saga of Silver Town," "Bad Men of Rimrock," "The Holy Terror," "The Chase," and "Indian War Party."

Viewers should be aware that these shows were filmed in the 1950s. Portrayals of Indians were blushingly stereotyped. "Fight for Geronimo" and "Indian War Party" are examples of that. However, the fight between Jocko and Dick, who was doubling Rodd Redwing in "Indian War Party," makes up for it in that show.

Episodes of *The Range Rider* were filmed two per week. It is entertaining to look at the casts and try to figure out by the personnel which episodes were filmed during the same week. Individual shows must be watched for this. Cast listings are not always accurate.

If one actor or actress only made two episodes, the pairing was easy, unless the entire rest of the cast was different. Trying to determine by the regulars was useless, as a number made multiple shows. Nevertheless, it was a great deal of fun trying to match these.

Though some are obvious; others were paired by process of elimination, such as the first two pairs listed here. With "Gun Point" missing and therefore unable to be viewed, it is possible that it would plainly be a pair with one of the other three.

"Gun Point" and "The Baron of Broken Bow"

Both are early episodes and no other cast is the same as "The Baron of Broken Bow" so these are likely a pair.

Only a few of the same actors are in "Secret of the Red Raven" and "Outlaw Masquerade." They were matched by process of elimination.

A listing of the paired episodes follows.

"The Range Rider" and "The Secret Lode"

"Six Gun Party" and "Gunslinger in Paradise"

"The Crooked Fork" and "Stage to Rainbow's End"

"Right of Way" and "Western Fugitive"

"Bad Medicine" and "Pack Rat"
"The Grand Fleece" and "The Golden Peso"
"The Flying Arrow" and "Hidden Gold"
"Dead Man's Shoe" and "The Hawk"
"Diablo Pass" and "Last of the Pony Express"
"Marked for Death" and "Ten Thousand Reward"
"False Trail" and "Indian Sign"
"The Ghost of Poco Loco" and "Harsh Reckoning"
"Sealed Justice" and "Gunman's Game"
"Marked Bullets" and "Red Jack"
"The Fatal Bullet" and "The Blind Trail"
"Dim Trails" and "Shotgun Stage"
"Big Medicine Man" and "Rustler's Range"
"Blind Canyon" and "The Bandit Stallion"
"Trail of the Lawless" and "Pale Horse"
"Fight Town" and "Gold Fever"
"Jimmy the Kid" and "Renegade Ranch"
"Law of the Frontier" and "Let 'Er Buck"
"The Silver Blade" and "Romeo Goes West"
"Peace Pipe" and "Border Trouble"
"Greed Rides the Range" and "Outlaw's Double"
"Gold Hill" and "Feud at Friendship City"
"The Secret of Superstition Peak" and "Western Edition"
"Ambush in Coyote Canyon" and "Saga of Silver Town"
"Indian War Party" and "Cherokee Round-Up"
"Bad Men of Rimrock" and "Outlaw Territory"
"Treasure of Santa Dolores" and "Old Timer's Trail"
"The Holy Terror" and "West of Cheyenne"
"Border City Affair" and "Bullets and Badmen"
"The Black Terror" and "Hideout"
"Marshal from Madero" and "Convict at Large"
"The Buckskin" and "The Chase"
"Two-Fisted Justice" and "Outlaw Pistols"

The *Buffalo Bill, Jr.* episodes were also filmed two per week, but the pairings are less plain, as a number of players only appeared once.

# Index of Episodes

# Index